Buddhism for Everyday Life

Buddhism for Everyday Life

*Memorable Dharma Messages
from a Long Spiritual Journey*

Nikkyo Niwano

translated by
Susan Murata

with a foreword by
Gene Reeves

Kosei Publishing Co. • Tokyo

The cover shows Rev. Nikkyo Niwano with his hands together in the *gassho* posture of reverence, photographed in 1985.

This book was originally published in Japanese under the title *Jinsei kokorogake*.

Editing by Joy S. Sobeck. Cover design by Abinitio Design.

First English edition, 2011

Published by Kosei Publishing Co., Kosei Building, 2-7-1 Wada, Suginami-ku, Tokyo 166-8535, Japan. Copyright © 1995, 2011 by Kosei Publishing Co.; all rights reserved. Printed in Japan.

ISBN 978-4-333-02483-4

Contents

CHAPTER 6
BUILDING GOOD RELATIONSHIPS   •   75

CHAPTER 7
SUFFERING LEADS TO SALVATION   •   87

CHAPTER 8
GOOD EYESIGHT IS NOT ENOUGH   •   101

FOREWORD

Buddhism for Everyday Life is a remarkable book by a very remarkable man, one of the twentieth century's greatest religious leaders. In it you will find no heavy-going philosophical discussions or extensive explanations of difficult Buddhist teachings. What you will find are simple, yet very profound, applications of core Buddhist teachings to the problems and opportunities of everyday life.

The attitude and way of life that emerge most conspicuously in this book by Nikkyo Niwano, the founder of Rissho Kosei-kai, is what Fernando Tola and Carmen Dragonetti have termed "Buddhist positiveness" in their book of that title (*Buddhist Positiveness: Studies on the Lotus Sutra* [Delhi: Motilal Banarsidass, 2009]). It's a matter of making the most out of whatever is given to you, of approaching every situation in life positively. The title of the third chapter is "Making Change Your Ally," and the first titled section in it is called "Cultivating a Winning Attitude." At one point Niwano says that "the only way to achieve anything is to convince yourself you can do it and then go ahead and do it" (p. 128). "Those who can convince themselves that they will succeed against the odds are the most likely to triumph" (pp. 48–49).

This is not to say that life is without suffering, pain, and difficulties of many kinds. The point is, rather, that the way to overcome difficulties and difficult times is to look on the bright side or to find the silver lining in all such situations. By accepting the bad along with the good, we can learn and grow and become better persons in the process.

Buddhist sutras, including the Lotus Sutra, call this world the *saha*-world (*shaba* in Japanese), which basically means that it is a world of suffering; it is a world in which suffering has to be endured and, even more important, in which suffering can be endured and even benefited from. That is why this world is understood to be a special place to pursue the bodhisattva way of helping others to cope with their suffering. Thus, even suffering can be understood and experienced positively.

This approach is based to some extent on the teaching found in the Lotus Sutra and later identified as "buddha-nature," the idea that even ordinary people are potentially buddhas who have not yet fully awakened. "The core of Buddhist teaching," says Niwano, "consists of awakening us to the presence of this buddha-nature within ourselves . . . , an intangible essence that enables us to follow the Way of the bodhisattva" (p. 136).

Buddha-nature is in every one of us, often hidden or obscured to be sure, but always there, inside ourselves. This means, of course, that it is also within everyone we encounter or meet. "Stepping aside, opening the way for others," says Niwano, "is to acknowledge and worship the buddha-nature in other people" (p. 139). Acknowledging the buddha-nature in others develops our own buddha-nature as well as theirs. We help ourselves by helping others.

It is not surprising, then, that there is much emphasis on

interdependence in Niwano's teachings. "*Engi*," he says, is "the most basic of the Buddha's teachings" (p. 165). In Buddhist teachings, what this means is that everything comes to be in relation to everything else. We are never self-sufficient, independent individuals but live in a world in which no one lives in a vacuum or can live without help from others. We live only by virtue of the support of countless others. In turn, we contribute to the lives of countless others. What has to be decided is not whether we are and will be related to others in important ways but only how. We should, Niwano indicates, always strive to support others in positive, healthy ways.

This interdependence is closely related to the practice of gratitude. We only are what we are as a result of the influences of others. Though not all such influences are good, they are what has made us, and for that we should be thankful. By embodying a spirit of gratitude, Niwano seems to say, we are more likely to live in a way that will lead others to practice gratitude. And the practice of gratitude will lead us to cease blaming others for our troubles and encourage us first to change ourselves, our own attitudes and behavior.

Gratitude and thanksgiving, in other words, lead to an attitude of generosity and to the practice of being generous, translated as "donation." This is the first of the six practices basic to the way of the bodhisattva and perhaps the foundational practice of all six. "For the layperson," says Niwano, "donation is the foundation of all religious practice" (p. 85). He does not, of course, mean just the practice of giving money or even time and labor. Among the most wonderful things we can give, he says, is a cheerful face.

Beginning with the first pages of the first chapter, "Treat Others As You Would Yourself," one finds a great deal of this kind of practical advice in this book. Though it does not read like a manual, one might say that the entire book is nothing but sage advice for improving our own lives and the lives of others. Frequently discussed are issues of child rearing and discipline; practicing compassion in the form of small kindnesses in everyday life; greeting others on meeting and parting; the importance of giving praise, recognition, and encouragement to others; workplace behavior, including reprimanding with compassion; taking a positive approach to getting old; understanding death as a kind of transition to another life and to everlasting value.

He says in one place: "You may think your boss does not like you. If you make an effort to arrive at work ten minutes early every day and greet your boss with a cheery 'Good morning,' your boss's attitude toward you is bound to change" (p. 96). That's an example of the kind of down-to-earth yet profoundly wise advice found on nearly every page of this book.

This emphasis on the practical does not mean, however, that traditional Buddhist doctrine and teachings are neglected or ignored. While there are no long discussions, many basic Buddhist teachings are taught in the process of giving practical advice: the Four Noble Truths, especially the matter of suffering and the causes of suffering; interdependence, sometimes called "dependent origination"; the three distinguishing marks of the Buddha Dharma (here called "the three characteristics of the Dharma"), that is, impermanence or transience, nonself, and nirvana is quiescence; the six transcendental practices or perfections; the three poisons of greed or sensual desire, anger or ill will, and ignorance or foolishness; even somewhat esoteric *tathagata-garbha* doctrine and Yogacara analysis of mind.

But in no case, with the possible exception of the exposition of Yogacara teachings, are any of these ideas pursued for the sake of intellectual exercise. Rather, they are raised in relation to common, everyday issues in order to shed light on how we might better live our lives by making better use of opportunities given to us.

These traditional doctrines are not necessarily understood in traditional ways. The idea of nonself, for example, is not treated here as a ridiculous idea that we don't have selves in any sense but is understood, rather, to be a matter of inappropriate self-centeredness. "Look at yourself with a calm and critical eye," Niwano writes, "and you will see how wrong you are to think that everything revolves around you and solely you" (p. 78). Thus a potentially baffling doctrine is taught here in a very practical way.

Niwano was Japanese, and to some degree the background of the teachings in this book is Japan and Japanese life. For example, for Niwano, and apparently for Japanese in general, an intentional greeting at the beginning of the day is more important than one at the closing of the day, whereas in my own experience in America, saying good night and even embracing one's loved ones before retiring for the night is assumed to be more important. The important thing, I believe, and I think Niwano would have agreed, is that we greet each other warmly in whatever ways are appropriate to one's particular culture. And, usually at least, there is no reason why both morning and evening greetings cannot be observed in the same household.

Niwano draws on Japanese customs and ways of life and refers to Japanese problems, but less than one might expect. Of rural background, Niwano did not learn to use languages other than Japanese. Nevertheless, he learned to communicate well with a great many who had no knowledge of the Japanese language. Always smiling, outgoing, and friendly, he could use both nonverbal language and interpreters exceptionally well, leading him to be, in fact, a very cosmopolitan man, one with wisdom based on an unusually broad knowledge of the human condition.

One of the things that especially impressed me in this book was the number and diversity of people referred to. Usually, such references are not long quotations but brief remarks made orally or in writing. By my count about eighty different people are mentioned, including doctors and poets, monks and actors, novelists and philosophers, businessmen and baseball players, scientists and Confucian scholars, and many others; people from Japan and China, India and Europe, America and the ancient Near East; people from very ancient times and people of today. The range of Niwano's reading and sources is truly amazing. Of him it can truly be said that he drew upon the wisdom of a great many traditions, cultures, and times.

In this book, what we might call his interreligious spirit comes through clearly. He cites the Christian Bible more than the Lotus Sutra. One chapter of the book is devoted to "transcending differences among religions." And he makes the very bold claim that "a truth of one religion that cannot be accepted by another religion is not a universal truth" (p. 33). But, while emphasizing what the different religions have in common and the importance of interreligious cooperation for world peace, his is not a simplistic equating of all religions with each other. He recognizes that there are important differences between the religions, writing, for example, "The starting point of Christianity is the concept of original sin, while the springboard to understanding Buddhism is to look directly at our suffering" (p. 93).

It has sometimes been said that Buddhists are only concerned about relatively private matters, but here we find Niwano insightfully addressing a variety of contemporary social issues, including unemployment, early retirement, the divorce rate, bullying among students, and, of course, world peace. It is true that, like just about every religious leader, Niwano was concerned primarily with individual transformation and growth. He believed that change for the better begins with one's self and moves to the family, the community, the nation, and the world. But he was by no means unaware of or unconcerned about larger social, socioeconomic, and political issues.

There are a few surprising omissions in this book. For example, while there is a great deal in it about family matters and about relations between husbands and wives, there is almost nothing about Niwano's own family or wife. Even his oldest son, Nichiko, now president of Rissho Kosei-kai, is barely mentioned once. His other children are not mentioned at all. And while there are numerous references to the wives of others, there is perhaps only one reference to his own wife.

The Lotus Sutra as well is seldom mentioned in this book, only three times, and not discussed at all. And there is no reference at all to Niwano's own important books introducing or commenting on the Lotus Sutra. His book translated into English as *Buddhism for Today* has been enormously influential and important for many people, including myself. Yet it is never mentioned in these essays.

As said earlier, Niwano quotes from a very large number of people in this book. But one class of people he does not mention or quote is his intellectual antecedents in the vision and way of life that Niwano advocates so strongly. One thinks immediately, of course, of Norman Vincent Peale and *The Power of Positive Thinking*. Of course, Peale, too, had intellectual antecedents, especially perhaps the French psychologist Émile Coué of "Every day in every way I am getting better and better" fame. And there are more-recent well-known embodiments of this way of thinking and living, especially perhaps the popular American television pastor Robert H. Schuller, author of numerous self-help books and builder of the Crystal Cathedral in Garden Grove, California, with its popular "Hour of Power" television program.

Of course we would do well to recognize that it is not Niwano himself who chose what to include in this collection of essays. It is possible that a different selection of his writings would have included more of these matters.

Niwano was truly a modern Buddhist genius, a man of many talents and profound wisdom. Those of us who were given an opportunity to know him directly have ample reason to be abundantly grateful. Those who were not so fortunate can be grateful for this book. Some, such as myself, are doubly blessed, having known the man in the flesh, his warm and friendly personality, his constant enthusiasm, his firm handshake, and his ready smile, and also having access to his many writings, including this very helpful book.

Gene Reeves

Professor
Renmin University of China

Professor Emeritus
Meadville Lombard Theological School

Chapter 1

Treat Others As You Would Yourself

In the days of Shakyamuni, as the Buddha is sometimes known, there was a great Indian kingdom known as Koshala, ruled over by King Prasenajit. The king was a devout follower of the Buddha and, along with his queen, listened attentively to all Shakyamuni's teachings. One day the king turned to his wife, Queen Mallika, and said, "The more I think about it, the more I believe there is nothing as important in this world as myself. What do you think?"

I believe that the king was expecting the queen to say, "Yes, my dear husband, you are more valuable to me than anything else." But after much contemplation, the queen could think only that she herself was what was most dear to her, and so she replied, "Sire, I feel the same way. There is nothing in this world as important to me as myself."

"Ah, so you think in the same way," he said.

Although the king and queen held identical views of their own importance, they now worried that their deepest, most honest perception of themselves was contrary to the Buddha's teachings. After much consideration, the two sought out the

Buddha. Now, what do you suppose Shakyamuni said to these two?

It is, of course, just as important to value oneself as to value others. Yet we frequently encounter circumstances in which one must be sacrificed for the other; if we put ourselves first, we slight others, and vice versa.

After hearing the king recount his dilemma, the Buddha nodded and replied, "Majesty, it is impossible to find anything as dear to us in this world as our own selves. In the same way, other people hold their own selves most dear. The people who hold themselves most dear, however, must never inflict harm on others, but should hold them equally dear."

You may believe yourself to be the most important thing in the world, but if you think only of yourself and make light of others, you are bound to be hurt eventually. And if you expose yourself to harm in this way, you cannot be said to really value yourself. Furthermore, what is true for the individual is equally true for nations. At present, a country secures its safety through diplomatic, economic, and military means. But whatever the means, the underlying premise should be exactly what the Buddha taught: Value others as you would value yourself.

The Wonder of Fetal Growth

Our instinctive need for self-preservation is the greatest hindrance to achieving happiness. Clearly, it is essential that we be ready at all times to protect ourselves from harm. But this instinct often causes us to overreact, preventing us from fully using our inner power.

Look at your hand. Your five fingers curve naturally inward. Grab something and your fingers are reluctant to give it up. When we are desperate, our grip can become extremely powerful. But at the same time, the hand loses its ability to move freely and we become vulnerable to attack.

Often we refer to someone we fear as a "wolf." But what an offense that is to the wolf! Wolves may fight among themselves, but they never kill each other. Human beings, on the other hand, are not satisfied until they have absolutely destroyed their opponents. Our excessive desire for self-protection makes us capable of the most terrible things.

At the same time, there is another, quite opposite facet of the human character: our ability to sacrifice ourselves for others. We see this ability not only in our hearts and minds but also in our physical constitution. Our immune systems protect us from disease by attacking foreign substances that enter our bodies. Yet this remarkable system takes no action when a woman becomes pregnant. Half the genes carried by a fetus come from the father and are therefore foreign to the mother's body. Yet the fetus is allowed to grow within the womb for nine months. What is even more remarkable is that at the end of this period, the mother's immune system once again becomes active, to force the baby out of her body. If her immune system remained dormant, babies would stay in the comfortable womb indefinitely!

Do for Others What You Do for Yourself

I once knew a young man who had been a navy pilot trainee when World War II ended. He then aspired to become an artist and took any job he could find to help pay his expenses. This young man told me the following story.

In the confusion following the end of the war, he despaired more than once, losing all faith in himself and in the people around him. Thinking that there was no hope left for him, the young man determined to end his life. After wandering about looking in vain for a place to kill himself, he took an overnight ferry. He planned to fling himself overboard in the middle of the night when the other passengers were sound asleep. But as the young man approached the deck, he found someone already there, someone who, it appeared, was about to jump into the water.

Instinctively, the young man grabbed the would-be jumper from behind. "What can you be thinking?!" he cried. "You can always make a new start in life. You are not the only unhappy person in this world, you know. If you die now, you are only going to bring sorrow and pain to others." At the moment he spoke those words, the young man realized how foolish he had been to conclude that death was the only choice open to him.

"Compassion does not end with benefiting others [as you will be repaid eventually]" goes an old Japanese saying. I have heard that some people today wrongly interpret this maxim to mean that we should not demonstrate too much compassion for others because it will only spoil them. It is true that the more compassion we are shown, the more we begin to feel entitled to all the attention. But if we really think so highly of ourselves, then we should be treating others with the very same respect that we feel we deserve.

Saicho (767–822), founder of the Tendai sect of Japanese Buddhism, wrote, "To forget oneself in giving service to another is the ultimate in compassion." The Treatise on the Great Perfection of Wisdom Sutra also says, "Birds flock to the tree bearing delicious fruit." In the same way, people gather about the virtuous person who always thinks of the happiness of others.

When we think of others' happiness so much that we forget ourselves, we discover our own bliss. This is the most direct way to happiness. If you are running a business, for example, you will make all-out efforts to satisfy your customers. Once such efforts become thorough, you will be able to take pride in your job, which will cause an immense power to well up in you. Then your work can focus not on how much you can make people buy but on how to please them so that they will come back again and again. I often hear people belittle their company by saying that it is insignificant and unknown. But it does not matter whether the firm they work for is prestigious or not. What matters is the quality of their work.

Nishikawa Joken (1648–1724), a scholar during Japan's Edo period, compiled a set of guiding principles for townsfolk in a book entitled *Chonin-bukuro* (The Merchant's Bag of Wisdom). Here is one example:

> The merchant must at all times be humble. Humility does not end with being courteous to people, however; humility also is demonstrated by respecting the laws of nature. Business is more than using money to buy things and sell them at a profit. We must regard the heart of good business as a striving for balance. It is the true merchant who estimates the amount of goods needed, or trends in the market, and who does not make an excessive profit, but buys something where it is plentiful and sells it where it is short, and thereby serves the nation by distributing everything under Heaven.

That is the way of the merchant; and that is the meaning of service. The merchant house of Mitsui has experienced more than three hundred years of prosperity because it has never wavered from the way of the merchant and has always sought to serve its customers well. Another axiom, this one from the house of Mitsui, goes like this: "Business is like a target—aim at it with decorum and good order and you will not miss."

In this vast universe, people and things are all intricately interconnected. Do something to make another happy, and in time the same happiness will come to you. In the same way, if you are greedy, the consequences of your greed will come back to you.

Inevitably, anything you do with only your own interest in mind will not work out the way you hope. Strive single-mindedly to serve others, however, and you will become like the straight-backed archer with his feet planted firmly on the ground. When the archer's hand is steady, the arrow flies from the bow straight and true. Such an archer never misses his ultimate goal.

Give in Order to Receive

The Buddha instructs us to act upon the Six *Paramitas*, or Perfections, if we are to follow his Way. The first of these is donation. There are three kinds of donation. One is to give with your body, another is to give your money, and the third is to give your knowledge. Examples of the three methods of donation can be seen in a Japanese project to send fishing equipment to an underdeveloped country. Volunteers go out to sea with the recipients and teach them how to use the equipment. Another example is the surge of volunteers who rushed to Kobe in 1995 after the great earthquake there. These people gave with their bodies, brought gifts of money and food, and spoke words of encouragement to the victims. As these examples show, donation can be both physical and emotional.

The second of the Six Perfections is morality, or keeping the precepts. The precepts are not restrictions that bind us but, rather, guardrails that protect us on the Buddha's Way.

The third perfection is forbearance. This is not just bearing up under all circumstances but includes fostering a tolerant heart and mind.

The fourth perfection is perseverance, or effort. We must commit ourselves to strive diligently to follow the Buddha's Way.

The fifth perfection is meditation. We need to calm our minds by dispelling distraction. Think of a small building with six windows. A monkey inside peers through each window, one after the other. There might seem to be six monkeys, but actually there is only one, jumping from window to window. The six windows represent our eyes, ears, nose, tongue, body, and mind. The monkey that peers through our six windows represents the constantly changing state of our minds, forever distracting us. This is why we need to calm our minds and hearts.

The sixth perfection is wisdom. Wisdom is more than mere knowledge; it is the ability to see the truth. It is not wise, for example, to give more drugs to an addict who is suffering from withdrawal symptoms. Certainly we must have compassion, but compassion without wisdom is useless.

We must endeavor to practice the Six Perfections if we are to follow the Way that leads to true happiness. The word *paramita,* the Sanskrit word for perfection, means "to cross to the other shore." To do so is to travel from this world, so full of frustration and misery, to that other world of perfect peace and happiness, the world of enlightenment. The Six Perfections show us the sure way to make this crossing.

Many people believe that corporations and businesses exist solely to make money. No one, we assume, would want to operate a business that did not return a profit. But the ultimate happiness, the thing that makes life worthwhile, is to bring happiness to as many people as possible through one's work or business.

All the sects of Buddhism preach that we should strive to serve others through our work. The Tendai sect teaches that all our undertakings are the practice of the Buddha's Way. The Zen sect teaches that everything we do is an act of Buddhist faith. The Pure Land sect points out that even business activities should be thought of as carrying out the Buddha's Dharma.

Ven. Etai Yamada (1895–1994), the head priest of Enryaku-ji Temple and of the Tendai sect, had this to say:

> Don't think of work as something you do to make a living. Rather, apply yourself to each day's undertaking with the thought, "I am a Buddha." People who throw themselves wholeheartedly into their work in this way become indispensable. Such are the people who light up their corners of the world.
>
> If we live always to serve others, we will win everyone's respect. No matter what happens, let us be human. To be human means to go beyond the pursuit of immediate profit, to live instead focusing on mastering one's job, whatever it may be. Be earnest in your work and you will find you will earn enough to support yourself. This is what Saicho was talking about when he said, "Sustenance is to be found in the will to follow the Way; the will to follow the Way is not to be found in pursuit of the means of sustenance."

After all I have experienced in my long life, I truly believe he is right. The greatest joy we can have comes when we give freely of that which is most important to us, whether it is money or labor.

Even the miser who clings to all the money and things that she can grasp is transformed by the realization of what happiness she can bring to others by letting go and giving. Therein lies the merit of giving. To aspire to the Way that Saicho speaks of is to foster the growth and flowering of the buddha-nature that is within each and every one of us. If we apply our full attention to achieving this end, our physical needs will be met in the process. A bonus is that we will be able to accept everything with such thankfulness that our hearts and minds will always be full of joy.

People who seek only to meet their physical needs, who think only of personal benefit, will be so concerned about advantage and disadvantage that they will never have any rest.

Guardrails to Protect Us on the Way

Rules emerge naturally in a society in which everyone is interconnected with everyone else. "Do not kill," "Do not steal," "Do not engage in wrongful sexual activity," "Do not lie," and "Do not indulge in intoxicating drink"—these are basic rules common to all societies. In Buddhism, obeying such prohibitions is referred to as keeping the precepts. The five basic rules just cited are called the Five Precepts for lay Buddhists.

Rules tend to prohibit certain actions and thus seem to curtail our freedom. Many people consider these rules or precepts outdated and not worth heeding. But if we ignore them, we will wander off the Way and come to great harm. Only then will we realize that such precepts exist for a reason, that they are what protects and supports us, as well as society.

The Five Precepts are fairly clear, I believe. Here I would like to comment on the first of the five, the injunction not to take life. All religions have this rule. Societies have laws against killing others, and doing so is against all accepted morals. Yet there is no end to killing in this world and to the fear that it breeds.

"Do not kill" is also a call to value the things of daily life. Never should we kill another human being; we should also avoid killing all forms of life, plant or animal. At the same time, we should treasure the things we use every day. "What a waste," we say when a still serviceable object is discarded. Disregard for inanimate things eventually leads to disrespect for living things as well, and in the end can even threaten human existence. Just think of the way we have polluted the world and wasted our precious natural resources.

The Hidden Strength of the Humble

Buddhism calls the world in which we live the *saha*-world, a world of suffering and sorrow that must be endured. There is much we have to bear in living in society with other people.

Konosuke Matsushita (1894–1989), founder of the huge Matsushita Electric Industrial Company (now known as the Panasonic Corporation), once said to me, "I succeeded because I was poor, uneducated, and sickly." Normally we regard such characteristics as severe drawbacks. Matsushita was sent off to an apprenticeship after receiving only an elementary school education. He suffered from tuberculosis when he was still quite young. Yet he used these hardships as the springboard for launching the Matsushita empire and became famous as the "god" of good management.

Most of us lack his strength to take a seeming disadvantage and turn it into an advantage. We look at someone who is successful and sigh, "People like that always get their way. How happy they must be." But there is nothing as dreadful as always getting one's way.

"The greatest unhappiness a person can suffer is to make a mistake and never have to suffer the consequences," says an adage. When things go our way, we forget to obey the rules and become proud and arrogant. More than a few people have been ruined in this way. In contrast, people who encounter one difficulty after another learn to give their all to overcoming each one. At times our own inner strength takes us by surprise.

Accept everything that happens to you, whether it is good or bad, as being necessary for you at that particular time and place, and you will acquire the skill needed to turn a disadvantage into an advantage. That, after all, is the essence of humility.

CHAPTER 2

CHANGING FOR THE BETTER

We can drink water every day without tiring of it precisely because it is odorless and tasteless. Rice, bread, and potatoes are staple foods precisely because they are plain and simple. Water and rice—ordinary yet essential—should never be taken for granted. The truth is also mundane, yet integral to our lives, as can be seen in Buddhism's three characteristics of the Dharma: all things are impermanent, nothing has an ego, and nirvana is quiescence.

When the great tea master Sen no Rikyu (1522–1591) was asked to explain the essence of the Way of Tea, he replied, "Prepare the tea so it is easy to drink; lay the charcoal so that it heats the water; arrange the flowers as they are in the fields; in summer suggest coolness, in winter, warmth; do everything ahead of time; prepare for rain; and give those with whom you find yourself every consideration." Seeing the disappointment at such an ordinary reply, Rikyu added, "If you can host a tea gathering without deviating from any of the rules I have just stated, I will become your disciple." Soshitsu Sen, Rikyu's descendant and the present head of the Ura Senke school of tea, noted how difficult it is to devote oneself exclusively to one guest. It is not as easy as it seems to consider others' needs or to nurture the feeling of putting others' needs first.

The way one lives one's life has nothing to do with making a show of one's originality, bragging boastfully, or performing an action beautifully. For example, when preparing to meet an important guest, what do you do? Many people worry about failing as a host. And once they get caught up in worrying, they imagine things going from bad to worse.

This is true even of veterans in every walk of life. Even great actors can experience such stage fright at the first performance of a new run that it seems their hearts will burst—and until the curtain falls they struggle with insecurity. Musei Tokugawa (1894–1971), a master of the art of storytelling, said that it was so for him. It is also said that even famous Kabuki actors trembled in the wings when waiting to go onstage at the premiere of a new show. And it is well known that *chanson* songstress Fubuki Koshiji (1924–1980) shook so violently while waiting in the wings that her manager would have to first draw a special charm on her back, tell her "Everything's OK, now," and give her a little shove just to get her onstage.

The ability to imagine the future—as well as the dire consequences of failure—is perhaps one of the major things setting us apart from other animals. The deeper our fear of failure, the worse we feel. But there is no guarantee that worrying about something will ensure that all goes well. In fact, the more we worry, the more likely we are to propel ourselves into the very abyss we fear.

So Simple We Forget

There are universal truths in this world that no one can deny. Although the various things that happen in our daily lives may seem to have no relationship with one another, they are governed by the eternal laws that all things are interrelated and constantly changing, and that nothing exists entirely in isolation. "Well, everyone knows that," you may say. But universal truths applying equally to all existence, anytime and anywhere, are by nature ordinary, everyday truths.

"The greatest debts of gratitude," goes an old saying, "cannot be repaid." The air we breathe, for example, is essential to our existence, yet how often do we stop to consider this basic fact? Most of us take it for granted and do not even think about it. In the same way, we tend to take for granted the truths revealed by Buddhism. Yet when we live outside these truths, we cause trouble to ourselves and those around us. Shakyamuni commented on this: "One says this is the truth, but another says it is not, and the two argue. Why cannot people agree on the same reality?"

A truth of one religion that cannot be accepted by another religion is not a universal truth. What passes as truth in one country cannot be said to be universal if it is denied in another country. Neither can truth that changes with the times be thought of as universal. Truth must apply equally to all people, all over the world, at all times.

All Is Constantly Changing

Let us first consider the fact that all things are impermanent. This means that all phenomena are constantly changing; nothing remains in its original state. This fundamental concept of Buddhism tends to be interpreted negatively: everything, we are told, shifts and decays. People live a futile existence and are fated to die. In Japan Buddhism used to be thought of as bleak and pessimistic. Transience, it was assumed, referred to the brilliance of the moon obscured by a passing cloud, or the petals of the gloriously blooming flower wilting and dropping to the ground.

By his teaching of transience, Shakyamuni meant that one should not be distracted by fleeting moments of splendor. One achieves true happiness only when one is free to adapt to change. This teaching opens our eyes to the realities before us and gives us the strength to live with hope for the future. Since all things are constantly changing, clinging to the past only causes suffering. At the same time, troubles can lead to improvements. Bitter failures, in other words, can become the building blocks for future success. With effort, the poor can get rich. The sick can get well. Change holds the key to future possibilities. The truth that all things are constantly changing promises infinite potential. This hopeful interpretation of the Dharma is the starting point for happiness.

Do we accept change with hope or do we see this world as no more than a fleeting existence? It is not a matter of which interpretation is correct. Rather, they are more like the two sides of a coin. For the first half of life, we remain hopeful. In the second half we would do well to acknowledge the stark realities of transience and calmly accept the inevitable end to our own existence.

"How empty is my vow of absolute love," says a certain poet. The only absolute in this world is that all living things must eventually die. Nichiren (1222–1282), the eminent Buddhist priest who extensively spread the Lotus Sutra teachings in Japan in the face of relentless persecution, wrote that we should try to understand death before attempting to study other matters.

The doctrine of transience, in opening the way to future possibilities even within the limitations of inevitable change and death, lends us, I believe, the strength to give value to our lives.

We Are All Born Naked

I recently dined with a man involved in a wide range of businesses. "They say the economy is recovering," he noted, "but I do not see any sign of that. I may be driven to hang myself in despair at this rate." Just then I realized that the scroll behind him said, "Possessing nothing from the beginning." My friend had been joking, of course, about killing himself, but the bold words of a well-known Zen master seemed to hold for us a timely lesson. Saying, "It seems as if the Buddha has overheard our conversation and is explaining the Dharma for us," I looked at my friend. He looked back at me, and we suddenly started laughing.

That event reminded me of a similar incident I had heard about. Long ago a wealthy merchant who had gone bankrupt set off on a journey in search of a place to die. At a cheap inn he had just crawled into bed when he saw these words on a folding screen: "Born naked into this world, what can we possibly lack?" This brought him to his senses. "I started out with nothing," he thought, "yet here I am bewailing the loss of my fortune and thinking of killing myself. What foolishness!"

The Bible teaches the same thing: "Naked I came from the womb, naked I shall return whence I came. The Lord gives and the Lord takes away; blessed be the name of the Lord" (Job 1:21).

The Buddhist concept of emptiness (*sunyata* in Sanskrit) is a complex one to explain in philosophical terms, but Shakyamuni presented it in simple everyday terminology, telling us that our attachments are what cause us torment. It is because we cling to money and things, to position and reputation, that we suffer. We have all grieved at one time or another at the loss of something precious. It is at times like these that we should remind ourselves of our origins. Remember that you were born naked and will die naked. A human being originally possesses nothing.

I should point out here, however, that the attachments Shakyamuni referred to were those of greed, of excessive desires. He was not talking of the wish for psychological fulfillment or enhancement.

Leadership with Insight

The world is constantly changing. Until recently much of it was divided into Western capitalist and Eastern Communist countries; it appeared that the leading nations of the two camps, the United States and the Soviet Union, would be in conflict forever. Yet all that has changed. Russia has reemerged from a dismembered Soviet Union; the seeming monolith of Eastern Europe has crumbled into warring fragments.

The ethnic conflicts of the former Communist bloc, epitomized by the painful dismemberment of what was once Yugoslavia, are a sad example of such wars. The clash of people against people is not confined to one region, however. In the Middle East, Israelis confront Palestinians; in Sri Lanka, the Tamils and Sinhalese were at loggerheads. In many other countries, peace is fragile, threatening to fall apart at the slightest change in the local balance of power.

In contrast, Japan certainly seems blessed. Many of us assumed that our postwar economic prosperity would last forever. But prosperity, too, must wane in time. Nothing has made this clearer than the bursting of the Japanese economic bubble of the 1980s. The flow of change is an ever-present undercurrent of time. We go against the stream of transience when we lose the flexibility to adapt to change. The Japanese need strong leadership to guide them through times like these. To paraphrase the German sociologist Max Weber (1864–1920), what the world needs is politicians with passion, responsibility, and discernment. Those who can see far into the future in the light of the truth that all things are impermanent are the ones who best fulfill these requirements. People will happily carry out the measures promoted by a resolute and just leader but will not budge for an unjust leader, whatever he may urge.

The quality of a people defines the quality of its leaders. I have heard that politicians were so corrupt in nineteenth-century England that votes were auctioned. As the public became more politically aware, however, the quality and moral responsibility of the politicians greatly improved. Good fruit requires well-tilled soil.

Respecting the Customer

It is often said that the completion of a fancy new office building can be a corporation's downfall. Sitting at their desks and working comfortably in such an atmosphere, employees are lulled into thinking that their company is invincible and, by extension, that they can do as they please. Such a small deviation in thought grows, unknown and unseen, into a great problem that can threaten the very existence of the firm.

The male peacock has a long tail with elegant plumage that he unfurls in order to attract the attention of the females. Of course, the longer and more beautiful the tail, the more the females are beguiled. Yet because of that large outspread tail, the male cannot see behind himself and so he is easy prey for foxes.

Are you familiar with this experiment? If you drop a frog into a pan of hot water, it will be shocked by the heat and jump out right away. But if you place it in a pan of cold water and heat it gradually, the frog will become very comfortable and not recognize the danger. Even as the temperature rises, the frog will make no attempt to jump out, and will wind up a boiled frog. Although this is a rather cruel experiment that I do not advocate your trying, I think that it contains an important warning for us.

Every commercial enterprise starts out working hard to build a clientele and win its trust. At this stage, the company spares no effort in actively working for growth. This task is difficult and time-consuming; therefore the managers of small companies look enviously at the big stores that have only to display a large amount of merchandise to attract many customers. But many large companies become complacent, assuming that customers will come to them rather than that the stores should serve the customers.

The Ito-Yokado Company is one example in Japan of an enterprise that started out small and became big. A tiny, one-room clothing store at first, Ito-Yokado eventually became the most profitable retail business in Japan. In his book *Akinai no Kokoro Kubari* (Thoughts about Doing Business), the president, Masatoshi Ito, has devised a motto enumerating three things that should never be taken for granted: "The customer will come to you; wholesalers will sell you merchandise; the banks will lend you money."

Ito-Yokado's employees are warned never to forget that there are plenty of other stores with products that are just as good or even better. Customers can get what they want elsewhere. So when a customer buys something at Ito-Yokado, the employees cannot help bowing their heads and saying sincerely, "Thank you very much." They also make every effort to keep stores clean and comfortable. The customer, in other words, must always come first.

Ito-Yokado shows the same deference to suppliers. Normally, as a company grows, it tends to become high-handed and haughty, expecting its suppliers to be grateful that it even deigns to do business with them. Suppliers may pander to the company, but they will not do so happily. If a better deal comes along, they will abandon the dictatorial company without qualms.

"Where are you going?" we ask a friend or acquaintance we meet on the street. "I'm off to my bank," he says. "I'm going to my grocer," she replies. "My" implies trust, and trust means belief. Such a person is, in effect, a believer. I cannot help feeling that this kind of trust and belief are essential components of a free economic society.

CHAPTER 3

MAKING CHANGE YOUR ALLY

The T'ang poet Yu Wu-ling ends his poem "Offering Wine" by saying that life is full of partings:

Accept the golden drinking cup that I offer;
Surely you will not refuse to let me fill it up.
When the plums blossom, wind and rain increase—
Of separation and parting, this life has its fill.

Every moment of life is a parting with the moment just past. Moment by moment, the present becomes the past even as, moment by moment, it moves into the future. In Buddhism we call this change a repetitive cycle of birth and death. Every moment is change. Whether the change is for good or bad depends on the encounters that each of us has with karma. An encounter is a situation that brings about some change in us, in accordance with our karma and the karma of each moment, which in Japanese is called *en*. When our encounter with *en* goes well, change will be for the good. When the encounter goes badly, change will be for the worse. Change is regulated by the strict law of dependent origination, which defines the interdependent relationships among phenomena in our daily lives. We tend to think of it, however, as something capricious and unpredictable, to be feared more often than welcomed.

Some people complain, "Nothing good ever happens to me. I get all the bad breaks." We all experience this kind of despondence at one time or another. What we forget is that the more despondent we become, the deeper we mire ourselves in misfortune and unhappiness.

Human activity can be divided into three types: physical, verbal, and mental. Of the three, mental activity is the most important, because the way we think, the attitude we choose to adopt at any given moment, has a powerful impact on events and on how they will turn out.

Cultivating a Winning Attitude

One of Japan's greatest professional baseball players, Shigeo Nagashima of the Yomiuri Giants, could always be counted on to come through when his team needed him. Asked the secret of his batting, he replied, "When I know I've got to hit that ball or we're going to lose, I tell myself I can do it. I picture myself hitting a home run and I do not think of anything else. Not for an instant do I even consider the possibility that I might miss." He has practiced so hard that there's no reason he should fail. When we have this kind of confidence, we can get through the worst of times. Nagashima worked hard to perfect his batting technique. I know this because some of his former teammates often visited me and told stories of how hard he practiced.

Change moves in whatever direction we wish it to. The more we hope for the best, the more likely it is that things will go well. If we want good results, there is no point in fretting over what might go wrong. This is the meaning of a positive attitude.

Kiyoshi Nakahata was one of the Yomiuri Giants' best batters. Once when he was working out, Nagashima—then manager of the Yomiuri Giants—strolled over and asked him how he was doing. "So-so," Nakahata replied. "That's no good," said Nagashima. "You must tell yourself you're in tip-top shape." From then on Nakahata made it a habit always to say he was in tip-top shape. He said it so often that he became known as the "tip-top man." The fact is, he really did get into good shape around that time, becoming one of the team's most valuable players.

There is no need to worry about whether good deeds will lead to good results. Virtue is acquired by constant effort. Do not misunderstand me: worry is unnecessary, but caring and consideration are important. Consider others, but do not fret over them. Do the best you can and accept the outcome as the response of the heavens to your efforts. This is what it means to leave everything up to them.

What Will Be Will Be

A long time ago in Kyoto I had the pleasure of dining with the first Japanese to win the Nobel Prize for physics, Hideki Yukawa (1907–1981). He was said to have thought of his prize-winning theories on nuclear forces and mesons (tiny fundamental particles) while in bed in the middle of the night. I asked if that were true. He laughed and replied, "The Japanese like tales of sudden inspiration—you know, how enlightenment was suddenly attained while raking the yard and watching the dancing leaves. That sort of thing." Dr. Yukawa's inspiration did not come out of thin air. He developed his theories after mulling them over every waking moment. His achievement was actually the result of considerable effort.

A story I enjoy is told by University of Tsukuba professor Masaya Oyabu in his book *Kokoro de Ikiru* (Living from the Heart). The head priest of a temple lay dying. "I've written instructions on how to resolve any major problems the temple may run into. You'll find them in a box behind the principal image of worship." A decade or so later the temple did indeed run into trouble, and the priests could think of no way out. Remembering the head priest's last words, they searched for the box of instructions and found it exactly where he had said it would be. They opened it in anticipation; at last, their problems would be solved. Inside the box was a note. Taking it out, they read: "What will be will be. Stop worrying." At first they wondered whether they were being made fools of, but gradually they began nodding, seeing the deeper meaning behind the words.

If things will be as they will be no matter what, you may ask, what is the point of thinking about anything at all? But "what will be will be" only after we have thought hard about possible solutions. Only after we have done everything possible can we sit back and let events work themselves out as they will. Simply sitting back and letting things go is the lazy person's excuse for doing nothing.

Learning from Adversity

"Reverend Niwano, you are such an optimist," I am often told. "What is your secret?" I have no special secret. I simply believe that anything can be changed for the good, and I do not waste my time worrying about things over which I have no control.

Problems are bound to arise wherever a lot of people gather

together. I have been involved for many years with the World Conference of Religions for Peace, an organization of religious leaders from around the world who have united in the hope of achieving world peace. The group has encountered various obstacles, but the knottier the problem, the more enthusiastic I become about finding a solution. I believe that there is no human problem that cannot be humanly resolved. How often have you worried about something only to look back later and realize that all your worry was for nothing? And how often have you wanted to shout harsh words at those around you, only to be glad the next day that you did not?

Suppose that things do not turn out the way you want. If you can glean a lesson from the outcome, there is something good to be had after all. The heavens will never burden you with more than you can bear. Many are the difficulties to be encountered on the long road of life, yet every obstacle has been placed with the assurance that you can overcome it and grow in the process. One day you will realize that the person you are now was molded by the trials and tribulations you over-came in the past. When we see things this way, we realize that there is no such thing as an unhappy or unsuccessful life.

To repeat, every trial is an opportunity to progress one step further in our growth. To take advantage of the opportunity is to believe in the compassion and mercy of the Buddha. In test-ing us, he is drawing out our hidden powers and characteris-tics. I have lived by this conviction and surmounted numerous difficulties that way.

In *The Miscellany of a Japanese Priest,* Yoshida Kenko (who flourished in the fourteenth century) wrote in the section "On Good and Bad Friends" that one type of bad friend consists of "those with lusty constitutions who are never ill." Although it might strike us as odd that someone who is very healthy would not make a good friend, such people cannot understand the suffering that comes with illness, having never experienced it themselves, and therefore tend to make light of the suffering of others. If you yourself have been ill and have experienced suffering, it was when you confronted your pain that you first understood what pain and suffering are all about. And sometimes the very act of becoming ill helps us understand the happiness that we had all along but were unaware of until illness struck.

Whenever I have a problem, I think that if I can overcome it, I will be able to understand and comfort other people when they go through the same kind of pain—that is why the heavens have given me this trial. Many are the difficulties I have surmounted that way. With this kind of attitude, one stops fretting about this, that, and the other thing. It becomes possible to accept the judgment of the Buddha with good grace.

Do Not Strike Out without Trying

Quite some time ago my secretary was using a machine that was supposed to test psychic power. I do not know how scientific it was, but you would push a button and a needle would move to the right or left on a scale. It was equally possible for the needle to go either way. The direction was ostensibly determined by the concentration of the person who pushed the button. The machine worked like this: you sat facing the machine and concentrated with all your might on making the needle move whichever way you wanted, to the right or to the left. Keeping that thought firmly in mind, you pushed the button. It was claimed that the percentage of times the needle moved the way you desired indicated your level of psychic power.

I do believe that a person's concentration can produce a certain kind of power or energy. In our ever-changing world, a person driven by a strong desire to achieve something can have a profound influence on events and people.

In 1979–81 more than fifty employees of the American embassy in Tehran were held hostage for fourteen months. The embassy takeover was initiated by militant students, followers of the Ayatollah Khomeini, in protest against the American refusal to turn over the exiled Shah Mohammed Reza Pahlavi, who was in an American hospital. President Jimmy Carter was quick to respond by sending the U.S. Navy into the Persian Gulf, but the ayatollah declared the situation a holy war, and an uneasy standoff ensued. A group of U.S. senators then appealed to the World Conference of Religions for Peace to intercede.

I was eager to help and asked the Iranian ambassador in Tokyo to arrange a meeting with the ayatollah. "Whatever the reason," I wanted to say to the ayatollah, "taking over the American embassy violates international law. You should argue your case before the United Nations." I was willing to take the hostages' place if necessary. Those close to me, however, pleaded with me to mind my own business. Getting involved was too dangerous, they declared.

It was during that impasse that the manager of the Nankai Hawks baseball team, Kazuto Tsuruoka, made a remark that was to leave a deep impression on me. Responding to a television interviewer's question about what would anger him most as the manager of a baseball team, Tsuruoka said, "You know that a hit now will turn the game in our favor, so you send in a pinch hitter. He swings with all his might but misses the ball every time. At least he tried. You figure the pitcher is just that much better. But it makes me furious if the batter just stands there and strikes out without even swinging the bat. I really give that kind of batter what-for when he comes back to the bench."

That's right, I thought. You cannot just stand there waiting for world peace to happen. You cannot give up without at least trying to hit every ball that comes, you have to swing with all your might. Make a hit and you have succeeded; miss and you still have a chance at another ball.

I used this story to make my point with my secretary and the others who were against my meeting the ayatollah. "You're right," they admitted. "Let this opportunity go by and we'll be wringing our hands in regret for the rest of our lives. We've got to at least try." After that, preparations went smoothly and I did eventually meet the ayatollah to plead for peace.

Having the Courage to Give Things Up

How often we just give up without even trying! We can feel so overwhelmed by the mere idea of all the energy and effort needed to achieve a desired result that we never attempt to act on our dreams.

I have heard that Riyoko Ikeda, author of the immensely popular "Rose of Versailles" comic-book epic, passed the entrance examinations for Tokyo Music College at the age of forty-seven. I was impressed when she said, "I kept telling my vacillating self that if I was serious about achieving this, I would have to give up certain things."

No one knows for sure that she is going to get what she strives for. No decision is hard if success is probable; the hard decisions appear when victory is in doubt. Those who can convince themselves that they will succeed against the odds are the most likely to triumph. When you confront a problem, swing with all your might. Do not let the problem just speed toward you while you squirm in indecision. Confidence is something you build up within yourself after trying over and over again. I would also like to add how important it is to take risks at certain points in our lives.

In July 1963, as vice-head of the Peace Delegation of Religious Leaders for Banning Nuclear Weapons, I visited several European countries and met Pope Paul VI. I have had a few similar opportunities to meet Pope John Paul II. I was deeply moved by both men's intense dedication to their calling.

I once commented to one of John Paul II's aides that I was impressed by how many languages the pope could speak. The aide replied, "The English words *decision* and *decide* come from the Latin *decidere,* which can mean 'cut off' or 'discard.' For example, if you are going to climb Mount Everest, you can take along only the very bare necessities for survival. Everything else has to be left behind. You will never reach the summit by adding one thing after another until you are burdened with too much weight. Mastering languages is like climbing a mountain; you have to concentrate on the essentials."

We Japanese live in an age of affluence. We want everything and seldom have to choose. We are so burdened with things that we cannot move one way or the other. So confusing are the choices before us that we have lost the capacity for single-minded concentration. We cannot let go of the unessential in order to achieve our ends. It is not surprising that some people claim that the heavens have punished us for our sins by giving us everything we could want.

Masahiro Mori, a professor emeritus of the Tokyo Institute of Technology and known to many as "Dr. Robot" for his robotic studies and his book *The Buddha in the Robot,* has profound scientific insight into Buddhism. For example, regarding the Buddhist tenet that all things are impermanent, he notes that only humans think of things as dying or breaking. When a flower withers or a vase breaks, we throw it away. Such things are no longer useful, we think. But that is a human bias; the drooping flower and the broken vase have, objectively speaking, only changed. Who is to say that they are no longer useful?

Take the instance of a metal plate. When it is shaped in a press, we say we are "making" something. But from the perspective of the metal plate, we are destroying its original form. In other words, creating and destroying are one and the same. You cannot create without changing something.

The head priest of the Tendai sect of Japanese Buddhism, Ven. Etai Yamada, often said in his later years that death was but one way to be reborn. Rather than being the fearful opposite of life, death is actually one and the same as life. What peace comes to us once we realize this fundamental truth! As Mahatma Gandhi said, the seed must die for the sprout of new life to emerge. Life also comes out of death.

CHAPTER 4

CHANGE MUST START WITH YOU

Some people debate whether there is any such thing as a previous life. But in Japan our frequent references to a person's "inborn" character and "natural-born" talents are an unconscious acknowledgment that an individual is the accumulation of the experiences and habits of his former lives.

Of course, we are not conscious decision makers at the moment we arrive in this world. It is only later that we come to assert ourselves. We grow up under the slow but subtle influence of the everyday behavior of our parents and others close to us. In time we go to school, where our teachers and friends help further solidify our views and way of thinking. There is no such thing, in other words, as a self that is not influenced by others.

Whether a person's disposition is inherited or congenital, it is molded by the people—parents and others—with whom that person lives for twenty years. Slowly but surely the self, both body and mind, is unconsciously shaped by these surrounding influences. Buddhism makes an analogy with the way the fragrance of burning incense clings to our clothing.

Our habits and customs are the accumulation of our

responses to all the things we see, hear, and learn each day; in time, they merge to form what we call character. This is what the ancient Chinese *Shu Ching* (Book of Documents) means when it says that our habits form our character.

When we accept the premise that we are greatly influenced by our surroundings, we then naturally begin to wonder how many of our preferences and decisions are really our own.

No One Exists Alone

No one can live in isolation, but we hate interference. We are inundated from morning to night by so many people and so much information that sometimes we long for a few precious moments of quiet alone.

What would happen to us if we were completely free of others' influences? An experiment was once conducted in which blindfolded volunteers with their ears plugged were each placed alone in a completely silent room. They came into contact with no one and were completely cut off from all sources of information. Nothing was required of the volunteers except that each stay isolated in one of these rooms. At first the volunteers slept, but they could not sleep forever. They began talking or singing to themselves out of boredom, and eventually they started to hallucinate. By then they were ready to be hypnotized. Asked under hypnosis how much two plus three was, they would answer five, but if they were chided, "But you know, two plus three is six," they would quickly apologize for their "mistake." Psychiatry says that such eagerness to please arises from the human intolerance of solitude. The experiment demonstrates how important it is to maintain constant interaction with the people and events around us.

To be completely cut off from the world, to be deprived of all stimulus, is to lose touch with our *en,* the continuity of people and things that defines our being. People left in such a state of limbo for long periods are bound to show signs of imbalance. Alone, with no place and no one to turn to, we begin to doubt our own existence. We cannot confirm our own being in a vacuum. The Chinese character-compound for "human being" literally means "person and relationship" and symbolizes the interrelations binding all human beings. Humans are social animals. Alone we lose our humanity—in psychiatric terms, we suffer an identity crisis.

Even as we grow and change, we maintain the conviction that, deep down, we are part of the same continuum. Losing this sense of unity plunges us into confusion. The self exists in relation to the people and things around it; we cannot live without confirming this relationship.

Debts of Gratitude

Everything that exists is constantly changing, but as I noted earlier, we tend to live as if nothing will ever change. In the same way, we tend to ignore the law that nothing has an ego; that is, nothing in the world exists in isolation. Yet how much more we would treasure the here and now if we understood the law that all things are impermanent. And how much more willing we would be to show kindness if we only recognized that we do not exist alone.

Certainly we are well aware of our superficial relationships with our family, neighbors, coworkers, and bosses. But we tend to see only each individual, remaining unaware of how closely we all are actually bound together. We are bound not only to those people and things most intimate with us but also, by invisible threads, to people and things that seem to have absolutely nothing to do with us. These threads crisscross in a complicated web of cause and effect, a web of existence that is constantly changing and that is the final confirmation of all existence.

One key to a happy life is learning to recognize the reality of our interlocking existences. We were brought into this world by our parents, who in turn would not exist were it not for our grandparents. And our grandparents owe their existence to our great-grandparents. Trace our origins and it becomes clear that we owe our lives to an unbroken line going far back to our earliest ancestors. Count the numbers and we find ourselves linked to tens of thousands of millions of people. Without even one of this multitude, we would not exist here and now. So you see that when we speak of meeting someone as a "karmic encounter," we are not so far off the mark: even a chance acquaintance is part of one's destiny.

As another example, take the clothing we wear. A woolen garment owes its existence to the people who tended and sheared the sheep, wove the cloth, transported the fabric, and sewed the garment. Go even further, and we must recognize the sun that kept the sheep warm in places like Australia and New Zealand and the water and grass that kept the sheep alive. One might even say that the whole universe has been woven into the garment.

Once we acknowledge that our lives are intimately related to innumerable other existences, it becomes impossible to insist that we can live on our own. We may have thought we were living under our own power, but now we see that we are supported by others. We realize that there is no such thing as an independent self.

According to an old Japanese saying, no human was ever born from the crotch of a tree. No baby can change its own diapers. Many of us do not grow our own food. We depend on numerous other people to meet our most basic needs. Awareness of that obligation to others is called *katannu* in Pali. Roughly translated, it means "knowing what has been done for you." Inherent in knowing one's obligations is a curiosity about why one exists.

No one can exist without the help of others. No matter how arrogant and pompous we may be, no matter how affluent, we must depend on others, from the moment of our birth until the very end of our lives. This fundamental truth must be the foundation of all our interactions with other people.

Earth Is Home to Us All

If I recall correctly, Mahatma Gandhi said that even the agnostic is religious if he acknowledges that he is just part of a whole. Most people never realize this truth. It is that lack of awareness that causes so much suffering.

The word *ecology,* used so often these days, comes from the Greek words for "house" (*oikos*) and "logic" (*logos*). Earth, in other words, is like a house, and ecology is the logic whereby everything on this planet exists in harmony. That idea is the same as the Buddhist doctrine that nothing has an ego. People who live close to nature know with their whole physical beings that they are not separate entities but are one with their environment. The Ainu, the indigenous people of northern Japan, believed that everything came from the gods and was to be shared equally. They took only what they needed of the flesh of a hunted deer and draped the carcass on a branch for the owls to eat. They also left meat in bamboo thickets for the foxes and badgers. We need to rediscover this kind of humility.

The woodsmen of Hida, in Japan's Gifu Prefecture, used to

apologize to the tree they cut down. They sprinkled rice wine on its trunk and called out loudly as they cut it down, "I shall cut you down now," as a warning to the god of the mountain. The ancient Japanese had a deeply rooted respect for all living things; they acknowledged and were grateful for the life they were given by all things around them. I think that this ancient perception is reflected in the Japanese translation of the English word *love* as *omoi,* meaning "to think of" or "to care for."

Far back into a distant past in which we did not yet exist, and far into a future well beyond our limited life span—forever within the infinite continuity of time—we owe our existence to so many people and things, too many to enumerate. Our existence is closely related to everyone and everything around us. What someone else does or says affects us even as whatever we think or do must surely affect others.

Selfishness stems from a refusal to acknowledge human interdependence. And when things do not go our way, we become angry and suffer. "No carpenter," goes an old saying, "builds the fiery cart of tribulation. Only the self creates its own vehicle of pain, and only the self rides this pain."

Gratitude wells up within us when we realize how we are supported by those around us. Once we become aware of how much we owe to everyone else, we cannot help beginning to think first of others and changing the way we live. Suddenly the world is brighter and everything seems to work out for the best. We become like the car that has been struggling to make its way over a rough and rocky road; suddenly we hit pavement and the going is smooth as silk. We do not achieve this all by ourselves. We owe such happy change to the warm support of others.

The Japanese concept of karmic connection expressed in the word *en* is believed to come from the Sanskrit word *pratyaya,* which has been translated into English as "belief," "faith," or "proof." It is incumbent on us to strive to make all the *en,* or connections in our lives, good connections. And the only way to do that is to prove our faith and sincerity.

No matter what our work, the most important thing is to apply ourselves with single-minded conviction. For example, by responding to a customer's complaint with one's whole mind and heart, we win greater trust than before. Experienced workers see customer complaints as a chance to really prove their worth. This same kind of thinking is what defines the good leader. People will gladly follow a person whose motives are sincere and pure.

A renowned fifteenth-century Buddhist priest, Rennyo, rightly observed that it is easy to see others' failings but that we can be blind to our own. A famous proverb says the same thing: "You cannot awaken others if you yourself are asleep." We cannot move others if we do not first mend our own ways. It is said that Abraham Lincoln felt that after the age of forty a man was responsible for his own face. We would do well, in our forties, to concentrate our energies on remolding our own character.

What Moves People

If the social environment in which we live is out of balance, we must take the steps necessary to effect change. But we cannot do so simply by focusing our attention on outward manifestations—society cannot be changed in that way.

When the lenses of our glasses fog up and we cannot see clearly, we take out a handkerchief and wipe them. But if that handkerchief is soiled, we just make things worse. So we first have to wash our handkerchiefs, and then we can clean our lenses with them. It is the same when we want to bring about some change in society. We must not simply criticize society, but rather work hard on refining ourselves, on clearing our vision, on adjusting our way of thinking; then we can forge our own path.

In recalling the Vietnam War, General William Westmoreland noted that although Americans were able to capture territory, they never captured the hearts of the Vietnamese people. As someone astutely said, "Social systems can be nationalized, but people's hearts and minds cannot."

One's decision to participate in an activity is often based on who else is involved rather than on the nature of the activity itself. "If he's going to do it," we think, "so will I. If that person is involved, it can't go wrong."

Toshio Doko (1896–1988), one of Japan's most influential business leaders, promoted a number of administrative reforms. He was neither a government minister nor a legislator, neither a politician nor a bureaucrat, yet his single-minded devotion to reforming government administration inspired many others. "He made us feel that this was something that just had to get done," says Hiroshi Kato, president of the Chiba University of Commerce, a professor emeritus of Keio University, and the chairman of the fourth Committee on Administrative Reform.

Doko and his wife lived frugally, eating little and squandering nothing, and he poured much of his income into the school founded by his mother. He did not even own a television set. Some questioned the leadership of a man who rarely watched the world news on television, but Kato claims that it was Doko's solid integrity that won him the Japanese people's trust and that enabled him to push the government to institute difficult measures.

Clearly, good leadership makes all the difference. And a good leader is, in short, a virtuous leader.

Making the Most of New Encounters

Japanese companies routinely reorganize and reassign personnel at the beginning of a new fiscal year. Employees do not always welcome that change; many prefer to stick to the old routines. And it would seem more efficient to allow people to continue doing the tasks with which they are most familiar. Only if a move is a clear promotion is it welcomed; even then some employees insist that they would rather quit than change. Yet without periodic change we become creatures of habit, unable to grow and mature. The willingness to accept change as an opportunity to grow and find new happiness is what makes for good and happy encounters.

In his book *Mittsu Home, Futatsu Shikaru Jinzai Ikusei* (Praise Thrice and Scold Twice to Foster Someone's Potential), Sakio Sakagawa sees nothing wrong with temporary transfers and reassignments.

There are people who equate temporary transfers, reassignments, or apparent demotions with exile to remote hardship posts, like Sado or Kofu in the Edo period [1600–1868]. But management generally knows what it is doing. It knows who will grow and who will not as a result of such change. Reassignment is one kind of *en*. What seems a crisis can, if one changes one's perspective, be interpreted as a golden opportunity. Transfers, reassignments, or demotions may mean farewell to a comfortable routine in a familiar setting, but they also mean new challenges and a chance to stand out from the crowd. The company has set the stage, as it were, to allow a try for a comeback. This is what is meant by making the best use of one's *en*. Reassignments and transfers are unavoidable in the business world. Since that is the case, one should take every opportunity to shine.

Sakagawa has described perfectly the Buddhist injunction to make the most of our *en,* of the continuity within which we exist. We atrophy when we do not use our physical and mental powers. Few know this better than the astronauts. In zero gravity there is little need for muscle. In space too long, muscles become too weak to sustain bones. On returning to Earth, one astronaut nearly dropped the bouquet of flowers he received in welcome, it seemed so heavy. When the first Japanese woman in space, Chiaki Mukai, returned to Earth, one of her first comments was, "I now know how heavy a piece of paper is." How many of us even think of the weight of a piece of paper? Yet after just two weeks of zero gravity, her muscles had become so weak that even a piece of paper seemed heavy. No amount of rigorous training beforehand can stop the degeneration of muscle.

Hard labor is something we all want to avoid. But if we refuse the occasional burden and insist on doing only easy tasks, we weaken ourselves and make it impossible to develop and mature.

I have enjoyed enlightening conversations with such sports figures as former Yomiuri Giants manager Tetsuharu Kawakami and former Yakult Swallows manager Junzo Sekine, now a baseball commentator. I also learned that the former Nankai Hawks manager Kazuto Tsuruoka has his own philosophy about fostering the growth and development of human resources. I will never forget what I read about him in Keinosuke Kanei's book

Hitokoto no Chigai (One Word Makes All the Difference). Tsuruoka made a point of visiting the parents of every rookie, even in remote mountain villages. If after a few years that rookie became a first-string player, whenever he made a serious error Tsuruoka would call him into his office. The player might think he was headed back to training camp and enter the room in fear and trepidation. But instead of scolding the player, Tsuruoka would ask, "How's your mother?" This question was so unexpected that some players would burst into tears. The whole point of meeting a player's parents, Tsuruoka said, was to be able to ask that simple but disarming question. What a wonderful example of making the most of one's encounters!

CHAPTER 5

PARENT AND CHILD:
JOINED BY AN INVISIBLE THREAD

The brain cells of a newborn baby are like a blank sheet of paper. The colors they take on depend solely on the parents. This is the compelling observation of Noboru Higashi, professor emeritus of Kyoto University and a world-renowned authority on viruses, in his book *Seimei no Shin'o o Kangaeru* (A Study of Life's Mysteries).

The first three years of a child's life are a time of imitation. Incidents of the first year are deeply embedded in the child's mind even though the child will have no conscious memory of them later in life. Suppose the young parents of a six-month-old happen to quarrel in front of the infant. Adults assume that a baby does not know what is happening, but the baby does not forget. He grows up thinking that quarreling is what parents do. This idea is imprinted on the child's brain cells.

Babies who grow up seeing their mothers eating all the time come to believe that they must do the same when they reach their mothers' age. Parents often complain that they do not know how their children got that way, but the children are only mirroring what they grew up seeing their parents do.

A favorite recent topic on television is the family with many children—perhaps a sign of what a rarity such families have become. I enjoy these programs for the order found in the midst of seeming chaos. The children roughhouse, hitting and kicking each other, but after one word of admonishment from their mother or perhaps an older sister, they stop, exhibiting a refreshing respect for older family members. Japanese families are small these days, with only one or two children, or three at the most. Siblings have little opportunity either to fight or to work together toward common goals. As a result, many children show an alarming lack of empathy for the pain of others. They also do not know how to stop fighting once they start. Sibling rivalry is the proving ground on which children learn to become social beings. Without siblings, they never learn how to get along with other people.

Teaching Children to Respond Promptly and Clearly

Strict rules used to govern the relationship between teacher and pupil, parent and child. Nowadays everyone is supposed to be equal. Although a teacher or parent should certainly give children warm comfort and assurance, strict discipline is also important.

Bullying is a sensitive issue in Japan's junior high schools, but some people claim that bullying is equally pervasive in the adult world and that children might as well get used to it at an early age. I think that today's relationships between parents and children, or teachers and their students, have become too cozy, like those between friendly classmates. But the increase in bullying among children in elementary and junior high schools is, I believe, related to the lack of a model of good human relations, which does not develop until we encounter the vicissitudes of life.

Bullying has been an issue for more than a decade, and the targets are not only children but even teachers and old people. This problem has its origin in the family, school, and society as a whole. Accountability is multiple and complex. We are all responsible—parents, teachers, our whole social system. Those who cannot find sufficient recognition of their worth at home and at school are the most likely to take out their frustrations on the weak. Bullying becomes a way to feel whole. Parents must teach their children early to distinguish right from wrong. Bullying must never be allowed; children should be warned that their parents will only scorn a bully.

It is very clear what principles we should instill in our children. My eldest son, Nichiko, the president of the Buddhist organization Rissho Kosei-kai, often quotes Nobuzo Mori (1888–1966), a leading educator and philosopher he admires. Mori asserted that children's upbringing, based on discipline, is the foundation of all education. From Mori's book *Katei Kyoiku Nijuikka-jo* (Twenty-One Articles of Family Education), my son cites three things that we should teach our children. The first is always to greet their parents on waking every morning, and always to respond promptly and clearly whenever called. The second is always to line up their shoes after they have taken them off (in Western homes, this might be comparable to not leaving their dirty clothes in a pile on the floor). The third is always to push their chairs back into place beneath the table or desk when getting up. It is by following these three principles that children learn the basics of being responsible human beings.

These days, however, I hear that many children do not respond when their parents call. Such a thing was unthinkable when I was a child. My own parents taught me always to respond promptly when called. A quick "yes" to a parent's call, says Mori, constitutes the discipline of ridding oneself of self-centeredness. Neatness is also very basic in all of our activities. I agree with Mori that simple habits such as these foster a wholesome family life.

Discipline: Stitches in the Fabric of Character

Before Japan's recent prosperity, economic life was not so bountiful; children could not always have what they wanted. They worked at their play, making their own toys out of whatever was available, unlike today's children, who all too often have things given to them even before they ask.

An elementary school teacher reports that when he takes his pupils on an outing to a river, few of the children choose to jump in and cavort. Most seem not to feel the lure of the water, preferring to sit and play card games featuring popular television characters.

A psychiatry professor at Hitotsubashi University, Hiroshi Inamura, says that today's children have little patience or self-restraint. No wonder. A child will not learn self-discipline or the difference between right and wrong if parents only murmur a mild protest when the child does something wrong. All the child learns is that if you complain enough you will surely get your way. No one can acquire the character-building self-restraint of the mature person in this kind of situation.

Few parents in my day had much education, but they certainly knew what kind of discipline was necessary for their children. The basic premise of all child rearing is to teach children not to disturb others and to become useful members of society. Constant repetition of these precepts in childhood ensures that we absorb them with our whole being. This is the core of what should be taught in every home. No child who grows up without these ingrained principles of acceptable behavior can find happiness.

Certainly, we should never lose an opportunity to praise or comfort our children. Nevertheless, the occasional scolding is equally a sign of parental love. It may even be necessary, at times, to raise one's hand against the child who refuses to obey. This is what it really means to give our all in raising our children. The foundations of character are laid in the earliest years. Parents who complain that they cannot keep their children in line are only showing their own lack of character.

An authority on the brain, Michio Okamoto, says that much of the brain functions to extend the self into the outer world. Self-control, a function of intellect and personality, is believed to be regulated by the prefrontal area of the frontal lobes. It is this part of the brain, he says, that must be taught to realize that in this world things do not always turn out the way we want and that there are times when we must sacrifice ourselves for the benefit of others. "Education" of the prefrontal area of the brain is most effective through the age of three. Children of this age learn the disappointment of unfulfilled expectations and the occasional need to give in to others through playing and fighting with their siblings and friends.

Okamoto fears that, in comparison with earlier times, today's children lag in the development of the prefrontal area of the frontal lobes, which means that they also fall behind in absorbing the important lessons that life does not always turn out the way we would like, and that when disappointments happen we must learn to exercise self-control. We praise our children for the quickness with which they can mimic what they see and hear every day, such as commercials on television, but no matter how clever they seem, our children will not realize their full potential without learning self-discipline.

Children know when they have done wrong. Parents need to confirm children's sense of guilt and urge them not to make the same mistakes again. Too many parents avoid giving their children a real scolding because they do not want the children to dislike them. But how else will a child learn right from wrong? If you do not discipline your children when they are young, you cannot expect them to obey you or pay attention to your counsel when they are older. Teaching a small child to respond promptly and clearly when called instills a lifelong respect for elders.

Discipline is more than teaching good manners; it is the foundation of good character.

Scolding Is Sometimes Necessary

Life is full of trials and tribulations, and a child must learn how to overcome them. The Chinese character for "parent" is said to represent someone up in a tree looking into the distance. True parental love is best shown by preparing children for the future, not by lavishing affection and attention on them to the point of spoiling them. A parent should never hesitate to say what has to be said.

The lower mammals learn all they need to know during the few months in which they drink their mothers' milk. They depend for the rest of their lives on instinct and the lessons learned in infancy. A child also learns an incredible amount even while nursing at its mother's breast. What sets humans apart from other mammals is our highly developed cerebral cortex, which enables us to continue learning even after infancy. This is why child rearing is so important.

Proper child rearing fosters reason and good judgment. "The child is father of the man," wrote the poet William Wordsworth. We never forget the lessons of childhood. It is in the home that a person learns to strive for goals and to care for others. These lessons can be neither forced nor ignored. Parents who fail to teach them evade their responsibility.

The best way to teach a child is by example. Child rearing requires parents to have a firm grasp of how they want to live and how they want their children to live. Strictly adhering in word and deed to the morals and ethics we believe in is the best way to instill these same morals and ethics in our children. Fathering a child or giving birth does not automatically make one a parent. Rather, we become parents in the gradual process of raising our children.

Rissho Kosei-kai's Fumon Hall at its Tokyo headquarters is a multipurpose building with a stage and convention facilities, available to both members and nonmembers. Members of Japan's imperial family have attended events there, such as a concert by the Berlin Philharmonic Orchestra conducted by Herbert von Karajan and occasional conferences of the Japan Red Cross. On one of those visits I heard a chamberlain sternly admonish a young member of the imperial family. I realized then that even royalty can be taught proper conduct.

The former court chamberlain Minoru Hamao once told me that when he was entrusted with the education of the present crown prince, he was instructed to emphasize character. Whenever the prince refused to obey after being told the same thing three times, the chamberlain did not hesitate to spank him. I, too, have spanked my grandchildren on occasion. I have found that it won me their affection rather than arousing their resentment.

We must remember to scold our children out of compassion, never just because they have inconvenienced us. A sharp reprimand when a child has done what he or she knows is wrong can actually be a great comfort to the child. I have often seen parents nagging their children and yelling at them, not because they need discipline but because the parents are in a bad mood. Children are not fools; they know when parents are really thinking of their welfare and when they are thinking only of themselves. It is no wonder that children rebel. The parents' attitude determines the child's conduct.

Parents Who Lack Confidence

How many parents really pay attention to their children? More and more parents, I fear, see only what is on the surface. It never occurs to them that they do not know what their children are thinking or feeling. It is this lack of real concern that is the source of all kinds of problems.

A Jungian analyst who graduated from the C. G. Jung Institute, Hayao Kawai, said, "Compared with the past, many of today's junior and senior high-school students suffer from deep resentment." The problem is that they do not know how to express it. If they could speak up and say, for example, "I hate my father for being a drunkard" or "I dislike my mother for being so sloppy," at least it would be possible to pinpoint the cause of their resentment. All too often, however, even children with perfectly normal fathers and mothers are deeply troubled.

In the years before World War II, when all Japan directed its energies to building prosperity and a strong army, society's rules were clear-cut and parents' roles were relatively well defined. Society is completely different today, however; much more importance is placed on individual freedom. Fathers hesitate to impose their own values on their children for fear of harming their future. Mothers worry that perhaps they should not expect their children to follow the same path they did.

Children sense their parents' lack of self-confidence and are filled with a vague unease. Where, they wonder, are the guidelines they should follow through life? Their unease turns to irritation and they behave in ways they cannot explain. Some even commit suicide, never having been able to express their fears. If we are careful to see our children as they really are, said Kawai, we should be able to know what they really need.

Children Need Time for Play

Children who rebel, who dare to attack their parents physically, are most often begging to be saved from themselves. Our distressed children are desperately seeking help and relief.

Frustrated children are troubled at not being able to fulfill their parents' constant admonishments to study hard and succeed. They have no friends to whom they can speak of their frustrations, and their parents and teachers just do not seem to understand. All too often, they vent their rage on weaker classmates.

If we trace the source of bullying among our children, we confront the competition that rules society. Parents focus on the material, spending their energies on earning as much as possible with the least effort. We are so intent on achieving our own aims that we have no time to spare for others. Our children only reflect the same narrow-minded thinking.

The former director of the International Research Center for Japanese Culture, Takeshi Umehara, says that until the age of eight or nine, Japanese children are academically well ahead of their peers in other countries. But around the age of twelve, statistics show, their school achievement level begins to drop steadily, and by sixteen or seventeen many have become problem children. The same goes for the physical development of

Japanese children, who grow at the fastest rate in the world up to the age of seven or eight. Between ten and twelve their growth tapers off. It has been shown statistically that slower physical growth is accompanied by slower psychological development.

When children are between ten and twelve, their parents begin to nag them to study more. Children are not given the time just to be children, so intent are their parents on cramming as much knowledge as possible into their brains. Healthy psychological development is just about impossible with such overkill.

Umehara has pointed out something that I have been talking about for a long time. Every human being has the buddha-nature—the potential to become a buddha. But the buddha-nature does not emerge on its own; it has to be nurtured. Broadly speaking, the human heart has two sides: a buddha side and a demonic side. The two are always at war; the dominant one determines a person's whole being. There is no problem when we adhere to our buddha-nature, but all too frequently it is the demon within us that comes to the fore, often brought out by what is happening in society.

The troubling problems that plague our children's world are proof that there is something profoundly wrong with society and the way parents think. We have to acknowledge this fact before we can hope to save our children.

The Lack of Generosity in Today's Japan

A college professor friend of mine has this advice for fresh graduates: "I'll tell you the secret to success. Never forget to say 'good morning,' 'thank you,' and 'excuse me.' Be quick to apologize when you make a mistake. Abide by these basic rules and you can't go wrong." Of course, just being polite is not enough to advance one's career. But my friend has a point. These days, too many young people entering adult society lack the most basic social skills. Teachers are having to attempt to correct a situation caused by parental failure. How frail the modern family has become!

Four or five years ago, an American youth studying to become a Catholic priest came to Japan from Chicago. After he had been in Japan a while, he was asked if he had experienced any kind of culture shock. He replied that before coming to Japan he had been given the following advice by an elderly Japanese-American: "Japanese people will probably shower you with gifts. And they may urge you to eat all kinds of food. You must never accept at once. Only accept what they offer after you have said no three times and they still insist." Sure enough, the American youth was offered many gifts by the people he met in Japan, and he was often urged to eat all kinds of food. But after just one "No, thank you," the gift or food was promptly put away. "Was the advice the old Japanese-American gave me wrong?" he asked me. I found it hard to explain. I do not know whether refusing things three times was widely practiced in the Japan from which the old Japanese-American had emigrated. What I do know is that Japanese today lack the social graces they might once have had. It is true that many people in today's Japan lack generosity.

Terms like "family tradition" and "nobility of character" are seldom heard these days. Finesse and delicacy are learned at home. In this age of education and status-oriented material values, character building is more important than ever, and it is the family, the home, that build character.

This is the age of the nuclear family. Young couples seldom live with their parents. In the past, more than one generation lived under the same roof; family traditions were handed down from one generation to the next. Mothers taught their daughters; mothers-in-law taught the young brides who came into their homes the secrets of family recipes and the like. It was said that it took three generations to determine a family's taste for food. Each family's traditions were unique, tailored over the generations to meet that family's particular needs. Today we get our recipes from television and cookbooks, and everyone cooks in much the same way. Treasured family recipes have become a rarity. In the same way, family traditions and morals are rapidly fading, fragile flames flickering in the wind of changing times.

Not long ago a survey asked some three hundred families whether they said grace before meals. I was shocked to learn that only 25 percent did. I fear that the number is dwindling even now.

Chapter 6

Building Good Relationships

Love is a word of which many women are especially fond. Love is affection and caring; love is romance. It is a beautiful emotion. Love is to be given lavishly, but it can also be a source of grief and fear.

Inherent in love is attachment. In its most basic form, love is love of the self, and it can change at any moment to hatred. Love and hatred are two sides of the same coin. The duality of love is most apparent in romance. At its most sublime, romantic love can lead people to sacrifice their lives, if necessary, for their lovers. But this intense passion can instantly change to pure hatred if love is rejected. Love is a universal, inexhaustible theme, and innumerable love stories have been written in both East and West, and are still being written today.

We see our attachment to the self and to our possessions as essential to our being. But carried to excess, such attachments become a form of greedy love, an endless lust for more, no matter how much we already have. An analogy is the castaway in midocean who drinks seawater; however much he drinks, his thirst is never assuaged. The saltwater only increases his distress and hastens his death.

Freeing Ourselves from the Demands of Immoderate Love

The Sanskrit word for that kind of excessive love is *tanha*. True peace of both body and mind is achieved only when we are released from the demands of immoderate love. This is the state of nirvana—quiescence and perfect peace.

Of course, not all desire is bad. In Sanskrit *nirvana* means "to blow out the flame of desire." Yet as long as we live, we cannot extinguish the flames of all of our desires. What, then, are we to do? We need to learn to control our desires. We need to practice moderation, to tame our wants in the same way that a lion tamer controls a lion. Such control is perhaps better expressed by the Pali term *nirodha,* which means "to suppress." In the *Dhammapada* the Buddha says, "For the self rules the self, it is the haven of the self; so rein yourself in, as the buyer of a fine horse does with his purchase." We must not allow ourselves to be dragged around by the horse of greed.

Desire can be compared to mold; put to good use it can become penicillin or the yeast that enhances tasty foods of many kinds. What we must endeavor to do, in other words, is to channel the energy of our desires in useful directions.

If we forget self-control and succumb to the thirst of excessive love, we find that nothing goes the way we want. We are driven wild by hatred, spite, and jealousy. We live in an era that glorifies freedom. But simply doing everything we want to do is not freedom. True freedom is possible only when we learn to control ourselves.

The Peace of Release from Self-Centeredness

Romantic love is neither good nor bad in itself. It is, in Buddhist terms, morally neutral. It is a perfectly natural emotion but can lead to trouble when we try too hard to win another's love in return. A man may purchase a deluxe car and expensive gifts far beyond his means to impress the woman he loves, plunging into the dark abyss of debts he can never repay. And then there is the otherwise meek and mild office clerk who embezzles hundreds of thousands of dollars, all to please a lover. Excessive love can destroy even the most sincere and upright person.

At the same time, romance can infuse us with the energy to accomplish many things. In the desire to win and keep another's love, we are inspired to make full use of our talents. Many are the people who have achieved great things in the name of love. Even if love is not returned, it still contributes to our growth and maturation as human beings because it teaches us to control our desires and channel our energy.

If we allow our desires to multiply, it is we who suffer in the end. But if we learn to control our desires—if we at least try to limit ourselves and frankly admit our own failings—we can find peace, a peace like that which envelops the invalid after a high fever passes.

If you are always self-centered, you can never see yourself in true perspective, as part of a greater whole. You have to step away from yourself to see your being as it really is. So said Zeami Motokiyo (1363–1443), considered the founder of classical Noh drama. I agree that it is very important to take a critical look at yourself from outside.

Being taken over by an all-consuming desire is like pole

vaulting. I cling to the pole of self-centeredness for fear of falling. But I will never clear the bar if I do not let go. This is how I see myself whenever I notice that I am becoming attached to one thing to the exclusion of everything else.

Myself in Others

We need to stop and look at how we are living. Our yardstick should be the principles of transience and nonself, the idea that we and everything around us are constantly changing and interdependent. Do so and you will be able to see the self that clings desperately to what it thinks is permanent, only to find that everything is constantly changing. No one exists in a vacuum; we exist because of the support we receive all around us. And it behooves us to support others in the same way. Yet we think only of ourselves.

Look at yourself with a calm and critical eye and you will see how wrong you are to think that everything revolves around you and solely you. Only then will you be filled with the desire to coexist in peaceful harmony with those around you.

Imagine a net with a thousand openings, one of which is you. Are you worth only one-thousandth of the whole net? Far from it. All the other openings in the net support the one that is you, just as you support the rest of the net. If the thread that creates the opening that is you breaks, the whole net will be affected. Acknowledge this interdependency and you can at last begin to think about what you should be doing for those around you.

We speak often of the self, but Buddhism also teaches the concept of the other—the concept of all things other than the self; in other words, all phenomena. This seems an obvious idea, but consider it in terms of the openings in the net: if the opening that is me is twisted, the opening next to me will also twist. If the opening next to me is pulled, I too will be pulled. I belong not only to myself but also to the other. I and the other are actually a single existence.

My extended self includes the other, and vice versa. The other exists within myself and I exist within the other. This interdependency must be the foundation of any kind of democracy.

The Lost Sheep

In the 1950s and early 1960s, there was much talk of alienation, the feeling of solitude in crowds. Back then, however, there were still family ties to which we could cling. Today, even a family might be nothing more than a group of strangers living together, their only link the common blood that runs in their veins.

In Buddhism, sin is *adharma,* or nonlaw. We sin when we fail to do what is human. Sin is much more than just breaking human laws. It is equally sinful to ignore the suffering of another, because we are tied together by mutual bonds of support.

The New Testament cites the analogy of the shepherd with a flock of a hundred sheep. If even one sheep goes astray, the shepherd leaves the other ninety-nine in the wilderness to search far and wide for the lost sheep. What if the shepherd decided to ignore the lost sheep and simply go home with the ninety-nine? In the New Testament, the shepherd who seeks his lost sheep is God. While most people would worry about the ninety-nine sheep left untended, God's concern is for the one that is lost. Consider this from another perspective: How much more secure must the whole flock feel when it is clear that the shepherd cares in this way about each and every one? Surely the whole flock will follow such a shepherd.

So it is also in our world today. Take on the burden of another's worry as if it were your own; cry together and suffer together. Such action wins trust and encourages others to follow the same path you are taking. The same principle applies to effective leadership in the workplace.

Bullying among schoolchildren is a painful issue in Japan right now. It grieves me to think that there are children who see suicide as the only escape from bullying. We are deserting our young when they are at a most sensitive stage in their growth. Think of the anguish of being abandoned by the flock, the deep hurt and sorrow at having one's call for help ignored. I think we can see here a society in which the mesh of the netting that ties us all together has come unraveled. In the old days, no parent would have stood by and let his or her child bully another. The parent would have scolded the bullying child and taken him or her to the victim's home to apologize.

Opening Hearts with a Word of Greeting

I recently read a newspaper article written by a mother whose eldest son refused to attend school throughout his junior high school years. The parents decided to place their recalcitrant son in a senior high boarding school. The mother went with her son to take a look at the school. She was impressed that every student they passed said hello to them. She thought that there, her son would at least learn to greet people "like a civilized human being." After one year at the boarding school, he came home for a visit. This young man, who previously had always stayed in bed until well past noon, got up at six with a cheerful "Good morning!"

The chief director of the boarding school believed strongly that civil salutations are the foundation of character. Daily greetings were school policy. At first many of the students resisted, but in time they came to understand how good it could feel to greet other people. "Every time I said hello to someone," said one student, "I felt released from the gloomy obsessions that had tormented me. And it was nice to be greeted in return."

Find one thing that makes you feel good and put it into practice. It is through this kind of action that we learn to live in harmony. We can also change others in this way. I know that some people question whether the actions of a single individual can really affect others. But do not waste time worrying about that; just do what feels right to you.

How many people wake up in the morning to hail their families with a cheerful "Good morning"? This may seem like a little thing, but the person who is unaccustomed to greeting others will find it hard to get that simple salutation out of her mouth. "I'll be laughed at," such a person thinks, and crawls right back into her hard shell of self-absorption. Even a simple hello will not come naturally without the right opportunity. The only way to get around this kind of mental block is to act instead of fretting over what to do. Give a greeting once. Then try to give greetings several times in succession. Then try for a week and then for a month. In time, you will sense a subtle change in the people around you. Given more time, you will suddenly awaken to the change that has taken place within you. Your heart and mind will be released from the rigid controls that kept you locked within yourself for so long.

The subject of greetings reminds me of a visit I once paid to the famed mathematician Kiyoshi Oka (1901–1978). He lived in Nara Prefecture at the time. At the end of a very pleasant visit I took leave of the professor and made my way out of his house. After walking some distance I turned around to find that the professor was standing and waving to me from the far side of a field. He continued to stand there as I went farther and farther away, waving his hand like a jubilant schoolboy. I was deeply touched. Behind the lean figure of the professor lit by the evening sun I seemed to see the radiance of the Buddha. He was a learned man and also a person of great heart.

We reveal our true selves most clearly, it is said, when we part. In Japan it is not uncommon for the owner of a restaurant or inn to come out and see a guest off with a deep bow. This gesture may be just smart business, but it makes both people feel good nevertheless. Every encounter should be treasured as if it were the first and the last.

Given the transient world we live in, we must hold most precious the here and now. And it is only in the spirit of the nonself that we truly hold dear our relationships with others.

Fostering a Spirit of Empathy

We are much too quick to criticize the words and actions of other people. No wonder they refuse to open their hearts and minds to us!

I have encountered many, many people in my life, especially people suffering from all kinds of problems. It is my experience that the best way to deal with such people is to welcome and accept them uncritically. Only then will they speak of their innermost fears and troubles. The way to get others to open themselves to you is by giving a broad, sincere smile from deep within your heart. Listen to what the other person has to say and show by your attentiveness that you care. Listen without judging; receive the other with open arms.

It is said that Andrew Carnegie (1835–1919), the American iron and steel magnate, excelled at making people feel that they could tell him anything. He was a good listener who could convince the speaker that he was really paying attention and really cared. The son of a Scottish weaver, he emigrated to the United States and made his fortune, starting as a railroad messenger boy and eventually becoming a captain of the steel industry. He appears to have acted in the belief that wealth is a sacred trust from God, pouring a good share of his riches into philanthropic work, establishing a university and setting up the Carnegie Foundation to support basic research in a wide range of fields. There is no doubting Carnegie's genius, but it is also clear that he owed much of his success to his ability to gather good people around him. Engraved on his tombstone are the words: "Here lies a man who was able to surround himself with men far cleverer than himself." He must indeed have been a master of empathetic sensitivity.

Words That Can Change Someone's Destiny

The head of any organization must be farseeing and decisive, and he must also excel at seeking out valuable human resources. The top executive who turns away good talent will rue that day. Sato Issai (1772–1859), a Japanese Confucian scholar, warned against employing only people whom one likes. "That," he said, "is like adding water to water; you cannot expect great things to happen. The good leader is judged by how well he employs people he may dislike."

Zen master Dogen (1200–1253) says in his *Shobogenzo* (Treasury of the Eye of the True Dharma), "We should learn that loving words have great power to move the world." We must understand that such words arise from the affection we hold in our hearts for others; compassionate words penetrate others' hearts, and can change a person's destiny. Dogen also says, "People in the secular world use loving words when they politely ask after the well-being of others." Indeed, Dogen's words of love can start from such simple greetings.

The Japanese word for "greetings," *aisatsu,* was coined by Zen priests. *Ai* means "to touch upon lightly," and *satsu* means "to delve deeply." The Zen master used *aisatsu* to question a disciple and sense how close he was to enlightenment. The disciple was tested, sometimes with mild comments and questions, at other times with great severity.

What is ultimately most important are the human ties that can be forged only by mutual respect. Someone with firm convictions will never have an identity crisis. Only those who have lost sight of their roots ask, "Who am I? Where am I?"

Praise and Recognition Encourage Us

The family that values simple greetings like "Good morning" and "How are you?" has strong bonds between parent and child and between husband and wife. Why do we, as family members, have to be so polite? some people ask. After all, we all live under the same roof and see each other daily. As long as we are grateful in our hearts and minds it should not be necessary to verbalize our thanks every day. But just as in the martial arts and cultural pursuits like flower arranging, form is important. Start with the formalities and in time the lessons will be engraved in your heart. The Chinese character for "learning" is said to represent a fledgling trying to fly by imitating its parent. Learning starts with form.

By speaking, we express friendly interest in people. That is why we should try to greet those around us and expand our circle of friendship by greeting more and more people each day. No one minds a friendly word or two. And we can never show what we feel about another person if we do not speak up.

Donation is an important Buddhist virtue. The Japanese word *danna,* meaning "master" or "head of household," is said to derive from the Sanskrit word for "donation," *dana.* By implication, the head of the household should be a compassionate, giving person. For the layperson, donation is the foundation of all religious practice. No one grows rice just for the straw; the straw is a by-product. In the same way, the by-product of donation is a decrease in our greed and stinginess. We do not give expecting to receive something in return. The *Shushogi* (Manual of Practice and Enlightenment) says, "Making a living and producing goods are nothing but [types of] donation." Those with insight will understand and accept what you have to give.

We do not just give *things;* we can also offer a congenial, smiling face, one of Buddhism's Seven Offerings That Cost Nothing. A cheerful face can be a wonderful donation. We frown when we have experienced something unpleasant; this is normal, but our twisted features do not make those around us feel very good. Medical research has found that frowning causes the liver to excrete adrenaline, which makes the blood vessels contract. Too much of this contraction can be unhealthy. In contrast, when we laugh, the skin of our cheeks stretches back toward the ears, stimulating the excretion of dopamine, a substance that contributes to good health. This is why we should regularly practice presenting a cheerful face. Another form of donation taught by Shakyamuni is giving up a seat to our elders. This is certainly something we should be teaching our children from a very young age.

Speak in a friendly and gentle voice and others will naturally be drawn to you. This is what helps create a circle of harmony. And you must be the person to start the circle.

Everyone wants to be praised and acknowledged. That is why empathy is an important characteristic of a good leader. Just think how encouraged a worker feels when the boss expresses sympathy: "That was really tough, wasn't it?" This kind of compassion encourages subordinates and certainly promotes productivity. Doctors should also cultivate their ability to express empathy. When a patient complains, "I could not sleep last night," the good doctor does not brush the complaint off with an "Oh, is that so?" The good doctor says, "You were not able to sleep? I'm sorry to hear that. It must have been a hard night for you. Here, let me take a look." Kind words like these envelop the patient in warm reassurance.

CHAPTER 7

SUFFERING LEADS TO SALVATION

Buddhism calls the world in which we live the *saha*-world; *saha* is Sanskrit for "land of endurance." Why do people in this world have to endure? Because, as Buddhism teaches, all existence is suffering. You may say, "Surely, we live in a world full of suffering. But I'm not suffering now. It has nothing to do with me." Are you so certain? I agree that with all the material things we have these days, most people may not consider themselves to be suffering. But just about everyone has a worry or two nagging at his mind.

Take, for example, the parent who frets that the children just will not listen. They will not do their homework, and who knows what kind of future they are going to have at this rate? What about the daughter who never comes home until the wee hours? "What have you been up to at this ungodly hour?" you rave, and she replies, "If you're going to pick on me like that, I'll just move out!" Every family has its troubles.

We worry about our health; we worry about growing old. There is no end to our worries once we start thinking about them. And there is so much that angers us, too.

During the era of Japan's rapid economic growth, many

bosses hounded their employees to work, work, work. Sales clerks smiled at their customers and put their shoulders to the wheel without complaint. But now that the economic bubble has burst, suddenly many employees are no longer needed. Many people have been laid off by companies that are in financial straits. With no place at the office, they go home, only to find that there is no place for them there either. More than a few husbands have shown symptoms of a phobia about returning home, which keeps them from going back to an unwelcoming abode.

Wives, too, have been affected by the sudden economic nosedive. Dr. Toru Sekiya of the Sekiya Clinic in Tokyo reports that some women are showing symptoms of a compulsive rejection of the "at-home husband." Among these symptoms is the refusal to cook dinner for a husband who comes home early because his company is no longer allowing overtime. Wives are frustrated by silent husbands who cannot even keep up a simple conversation, and mothers by ungrateful children who act as if they grew up without help. "Why," these women wail, "am I the only one who has to suffer?"

If we start to count our worries and frustrations, there is no end in sight. The ultimate source of our worries and anger is that things are not going as we think they should. That is what suffering is all about. The popular novelist Fumiko Hayashi (1903–1951) said, "The life of a flower is short and full of suffering." How true. When we reexamine our daily lives, all we can see is hardship, dislike, misery, and anger.

The Risks of Overconfidence

Life is not a bowl of cherries. The tides of life peak and ebb. We all know that at the best of times we should be preparing for the worst of times that is sure to come. Yet it is hard to remember this need when everything seems to be going our way. We cherish the illusion that now is forever; we forget the fact that life inevitably brings suffering.

There is a passage in the *Ts'ai-ken T'an* (Vegetable-Root Discourses), a collection of popular Chinese sayings compiled by the Ming philosopher Hung Tzu-ch'eng, to the effect that the seeds of joy are planted in the midst of travail, while the seeds of adversity are sown at the height of pride. When work is proceeding well and everything seems to be going our way, we become arrogant. We do not realize that this very arrogance makes us vulnerable and opens the way to self-destruction. Just look around: people and corporations that enjoy overnight success invariably fall on hard times within a decade or so.

The more accustomed we become to affluence and comfort, the less we are willing to work for these ends. Things begin to sour and we are quick to blame everyone but ourselves. "It is the fault of those around me," we whine. "It is the fault of society and politics." This kind of thinking only worsens our plight. At the root of our problem is our failure to recognize that the source of our difficulties lies within ourselves.

The Buddha's teachings on how to get rid of suffering are known as the Buddha's Way. The Buddha recognizes that all existence is suffering, and he shows the way out.

The Way Out of Suffering

How do you react when you confront something unpleasant, something that makes you suffer? Surely the first thing that comes to mind is how to get out of the situation, how to be rid of the pain.

But the Buddha teaches us to confront our suffering head-on.

Instead of trying to feint this way and that in an effort to escape, we should look straight at our suffering and examine it carefully to see it exactly for what it is. You cannot cure a disease without first knowing what the disease is. After it is diagnosed, you search for its cause. Every affliction has its cause. Once you know the cause, says the Buddha, you will be able to find the way to release and relief.

Knowing the cause is the basis of the treatment of the disease. Good health can be regained with the right treatment and medicine. The Buddha's answer to the problem of suffering is summed up in the Four Noble Truths, the subject of his first sermon after his enlightenment. The Four Noble Truths are sometimes referred to as "the elephant's footprint," because just as the foot of any other animal fits within the great footprint of an elephant, all answers are found within these four truths.

We begin by looking straight at our suffering (the Truth of Suffering: all life is suffering) and then tracing its cause (the Truth of Cause: suffering is caused by ignorance). Inevitably, we come to realize that we have been selfish and ruled by our passions, despite our buddha-nature and contrary to the truths of transience and selflessness. Once we recognize that fact, we are on the way to discovering peace and tranquillity (the Truth of Extinction: the cessation of all attachments and desire is possible) and learning how to attain this state (the Truth of the Path: practice of the bodhisattva way ends suffering). These are the Four Noble Truths.

We can reach the state of nirvana, which is peace and tranquillity, through deeply understanding the truths that all things are impermanent and nothing has an ego.

The Buddha was enlightened to the truth that the universe was not created and is not controlled by someone or something.

Instead, the creation, continuity, change, and expiation of the universe and everything in it arise from interactions between causes and their accompanying conditions, according to the universal law of dependent origination. Everything changes and is interrelated. Transience and selflessness are the eternal truths, the only truths that remain forever unchanged. We suffer when we lose sight of these two fundamental truths—when we cling to something, thinking that it is immutable when it is not, or when we think only of ourselves. We attain nirvana when we recognize our own misperceptions and act on this realization by accepting the Buddhist truths.

The story of Prince Siddhartha's Excursion from the Four Gates is a familiar one in Buddhist lore. Siddhartha, as the Buddha was known before becoming a mendicant and ascetic, had three palaces, each with numerous servants. Great care was taken to ensure that the prince suffered from neither heat nor cold; he moved from palace to palace as the seasons changed. He was raised to know only the sweet things of life.

One day Prince Siddhartha and a servant left the palace by its east gate. There the prince was taken aback by the sight of an old man, bent and crippled, barely able to walk with a cane. Most people tend to forget that they, too, are fated to become old and weak, and they look on the feeble elderly with scorn. Young people especially are likely to assume that they will remain forever young and that aging has nothing to do with them. Prince Siddhartha, however, was profoundly affected by the sight of the old man, realizing that he himself would eventually grow old.

On another day the prince stepped out of the south gate of the palace only to be startled by the sight of a sick person in great pain. On yet another day the prince departed from the palace's west gate. This time he was horrified to see a corpse being taken away on a plank.

Some time later the prince went out the north gate. This time he saw coming toward him a man with a radiant face. "What kind of man is this?" the prince asked his servant. When he learned that the man was a mendicant monk, Prince Siddhartha decided that he, too, wanted to become a mendicant, and left his home for a life of religious discipline.

This story teaches us how important it is to accept the fundamental sufferings of the human condition—birth, aging, illness, and death—and to avoid the pitfalls of pride that lead us to assume that we will be forever young and healthy and that life is eternal. Our birth into this world is itself a kind of suffering. And, by extension, the life we are given at the moment of birth is also a prolonged kind of suffering. Simply by existing we are fated to experience the basic kinds of suffering that proved such a shock to Prince Siddhartha.

In one room of a hospital a baby is born, while in another room an invalid dies. Elsewhere, an old person undergoes rehabilitation, struggling to walk with the help of a handrail. The emergency room is filled to capacity with people suffering great pain. All this goes on right before us, yet we try to avert our eyes from the dreadful reality. We know theoretically that everyone must experience these kinds of suffering at one time or another, but psychologically we deny the reality and try not to look at it too closely.

It is easy to speak of death, yet almost impossible to speak of one's own death. I hope that I will be able to depart this world giving thanks to everything and waving my hand to the people around me in fond farewell.

We Are Pursued Because We Flee

The first thing we should do when we suffer is seek the cause rather than figure out how to run from the suffering. Everything that has a cause will disappear after that cause is removed. The only way to seek the cause is to gaze directly at one's own suffering. And the only way to look steadily at one's suffering is to accept that very few things in this world will go the way we want them to.

When we are in trouble, we are convinced that we suffer alone. But even the most cheerful, carefree person bears the burden of thwarted hopes and pain. However light her steps, she bears a burden others cannot see. Even the happiest family has its problems. You cannot place a group of people with individual desires under the same roof and expect to have no conflict. Even worse, many of us refuse to acknowledge that we have troubles, very much like the drunkard who insists he is sober.

First we must recognize that we live in a society full of trials and tribulations. In Buddhism we refer to this awareness as "realization of the truth." The Sanskrit term for that concept is *satya,* which also encompasses the meaning "truth." This realization does not mean surrendering but seeing reality for what it is, in other words, seeing clearly.

The longtime actress and popular entertainer Chocho Miyako (1920–2000) once very aptly said, "Even the saddest tears eventually dry." This is exactly what I am talking about. The starting point of Christianity is the concept of original sin, while the springboard to understanding Buddhism is to look directly at our suffering.

"Good and ill fortune," goes a saying, "are like the interwoven strands of a rope." Life may seem like nothing but one trial after another, yet there are always moments when we are glad to be alive. In fact, many people speak of difficult times even as they give thanks for the wonderful happiness they enjoy now.

Some people think it is hard never to have enough money. A rich person, however, might suffer because he cannot think of a way to take his wealth with him to the next world. Here a couple lament because they are childless; there another couple weep because of the pain their children have brought them.

What is suffering to one person may bring joy to another; it all depends on how you look at things. This perspective is what I mean by realization of the truth. If we think only of the bad things, everything becomes a source of suffering. As long as we see life as either happy or unhappy, and as long as we pursue happiness only, there can be no end to our disappointments. This is not the way life should be savored. If we accept that life has ups and downs, suddenly we are able to see the germ of happiness that can be found in even the most painful suffering.

Life may seem boring to some, each day a repetition of the day before. But to someone like me, who has trod the rocky, uneven path of ninety-plus years of life, every day seen to its end is a day for which to give thanks. I am indeed grateful to be able to close each day's entry in my journal with words of appreciation for another uneventful day.

Blaming the Stone We Trip On

We all want to escape whatever is unpleasant or painful. No one wants to reopen a tender wound. But no problem can be solved if we refuse to bear the pain of seeking its cause. And when we seek the cause, we must be very careful not to pin the blame on someone else. An old Jewish adage very aptly describes this syndrome: "Someone trips and blames the stone. If there is no stone, he blames the slope. If there is no slope, he blames his shoes. People are apt to blame anything but themselves." Always, we try to remove ourselves from any serious consideration of where the blame lies.

You are one of two people walking in the street; you bump into each other. "Why don't you watch where you are going?!" you both exclaim. But wait a moment and think: If you were looking straight ahead and it was the other person who was not watching where she was going, surely you would have been able to step aside. Obviously, you must not have been paying attention either. You both get angry because neither wants to take the blame. The same goes for spats between married couples and wars between countries: each side is convinced that it is right and the other totally wrong. The cause of conflict is the refusal to acknowledge that one might be wrong.

I suspect that we hate to acknowledge our faults because we fear the scorn of others. But as long as we insist on blaming someone else, that someone else will be equally insistent that the fault is ours. Deep down we both know that each is at least partly to blame. If you are the first to let down your guard and admit this fact, your opponent will surely follow your lead. People can fly to the moon, but we do not yet know our own hearts.

Buddhist teachings refer to the suffering of being with people we dislike. It is difficult to have to deal with a person full of hatred and malice. What we seldom realize is that in some way, large or small, we ourselves are responsible for our encounter with such a person. Those who complain that they never seem to meet nice people are most likely never to have genuinely liked anyone else. People rarely dislike those who obviously like them. Take, for example, your boss. You may think your boss does not like you. If you make an effort to arrive at work ten minutes early every day and greet your boss with a cheery "Good morning," your boss's attitude toward you is bound to change.

Recognizing your own faults will not get you anywhere if all you do is berate yourself, however. The Buddhist concept of realization of the truth is highly positive: our suffering highlights our failures so that we may correct them.

Illness is a good example of how to do that. No one likes to get sick. But when we do fall ill, we should realize that we need to reconsider our way of life. Too much eating and drinking will make anyone ill. If they did not, we would live out our lives never realizing our own excesses. You might say that illness is a silent signal from the divine to reform. Whatever our suffering, we can learn to accept it with thanksgiving if we recognize it as a warning to keep us from being mired in even deeper troubles.

Suffering can give us new life; suffering can be our salvation because it sharpens our focus and forces us to concentrate on seeking a better way. Sir Walter Scott (1771–1832), the great Scottish writer and poet, described this phenomenon eloquently when he noted that nothing is so pleasant as rest after hard labor, no meal so delicious as one eaten on an empty stomach, nothing so exhilarating as good health after an illness, peace never so gratifying as after a hard-won victory. The person who finds no consolation in life, he goes on to say, is a person who has never experienced fatigue, hunger, illness, or difficulty.

Cultivating the Spirit

The Suttanipata relates the following episode in the life of the Buddha:

One day in the sowing season, Shakyamuni was standing holding an alms bowl near a field owned by a Brahmin, where hundreds of plows were yoked to oxen and food was being distributed among the workers before the plowing got under way.

The Brahmin said to Shakyamuni in a petulant tone, "Samana [Recluse], we plow the fields and sow seeds to obtain our daily meals. Why do you not also cultivate the fields for your food?"

Shakyamuni quietly replied, "Brahmin, I too cultivate and sow seeds, and thereby acquire my food."

Not understanding what these words meant, the Brahmin repeated his query. "Samana, we have never seen you cultivate a field. Where is your plow? Where are your oxen?"

Shakyamuni replied with the following verse:

Faith is the seed I sow,
Discipline is the rain.
Wisdom is my plow, and
Shame is the shafts.
The soul [mind] is the rope with which they are tied.
Introspection [mindfulness] is the blade and pole of my
    plow.

Farmers till the soil in the hope of a rich harvest. Buddhism endeavors to cultivate the spirit, build character, and enable everyone to live a worthwhile life. The Buddha's Way may seem difficult, but surely anyone who realizes that following the Way means cultivating the field of one's own spirit will be eager to undertake the task.

Ryokan (1758–1831), a Zen priest of the Soto sect as well as a poet and calligrapher, wrote the following poem:

> In every home, people eat,
> But no one stops to wonder why.
> If I say something about this,
> Then everyone laughs at my folly.
> But rather than laugh,
> They would do well to live by the truth.
> Then they would come to understand
> What I am trying to say.

His point is that people should ponder why they exist.

When I founded Rissho Kosei-kai, I decided to become a milkman because delivering milk each morning and night freed me for the rest of the day. I spent that precious free time working hard for the salvation of those who suffered. I am not averse to hard work, and I always ensured that my family was able to get by. But as the number of believers grew, more and more people came to me for spiritual guidance, and I found myself getting only three to four hours of sleep at night. I was unable to increase my milk deliveries, and it was not long before I was pawning my belongings to keep going. There were seven long years in which I repeatedly pawned, bought back, and pawned again my only formal kimono, which I wore for our religious functions and ceremonies. My pawnbroker later joined Rissho Kosei-kai. When I met him at one of our meetings, I thanked him for all those years I had been in his debt.

He only blinked in amazement. I am sure he could not believe that the head of his religious organization could possibly have had anything to do with a pawnshop.

When fellow members realized my dire straits, they all pitched in and raised funds to support me and my family. I was reluctant at first to accept what seemed to be charity, but I recalled the Buddha's teaching that cultivating people's spirits is just as honorable as tilling the soil. Ever since then I have fully devoted myself to Rissho Kosei-kai.

Chapter 8

Good Eyesight Is Not Enough

What, exactly, must we do to overcome pain and suffering? The first step is to see ourselves as we really are, to see how we live in interconnection with our surroundings. This is what the Eightfold Path calls "right view." Only with clear-sightedness can we understand correctly and make correct decisions, which together are called "right thought." This type of thinking enables us to get directly to the point whenever we communicate verbally to others, and that is called "right speech." If we say the right things, everything in life will fall into place spontaneously.

What, then, is clear-sightedness? Asked how clearly they see their surroundings, most people answer confidently that they see them very well. Seeing things as they really are seems so obvious that we assume that it is easy. But good eyesight is not the same thing as clear-sightedness. Dr. Masahiro Mori, professor emeritus at the Tokyo Institute of Technology and famous for his work in robotics and his dedicated study of Buddhist philosophy, has said, "Just having eyes is not enough to really see." He illustrated his thinking with the following story.

The U.S. Navy used to spend a great deal of time and money studying the workings of frogs' eyes. In the tense atmosphere of the cold war, the United States worried about a possible nuclear attack by the Soviet Union. It was imperative to try to create a defensive weapon that could shoot down any missile before it reached its target. This is where the frogs came in, because a frog never fails to catch tiny insects that are flying toward it. To the researchers' surprise, the studies revealed that a frog sees only what is moving directly toward it. As with other animals, a frog's retina reflects everything in front of it, but its brain distinguishes only objects moving directly toward the frog. The U.S. Navy's research made it clear that frogs do not actually "see" with their eyes but with their brains, or with their minds and hearts.

Humans also see selectively. An artist looks at a mountain and sighs, "What a beautiful mountain! I would very much like to capture that beauty." The forester notes that there are some very fine trees growing on the mountain; the hunter thinks only of the game that surely must be hiding there. They are all looking at the same mountain, but each sees only what is already in his own mind or heart. People, in other words, see only what they are interested in. The uninterested person would not even see the mountain, as if it did not exist.

Seeing the World Upside Down

In our morning and evening commutes, those of us who live in big cities encounter multitudes of people on public transportation or in the streets. But if we are not interested in them, it is as if they do not exist.

There is a Zen instruction that refers to a *tampankan,* or a man who carries a large plank on his shoulder. When he carries it on his right shoulder, he can see only to the left, and when he carries it on his left shoulder, he can see only to the right. Metaphorically speaking, a *tampankan* is anyone who sees only half of reality and is convinced that it is the whole. Such people think that they understand completely when, in reality, they have not grasped "reality" at all. What they actually have is nothing but superficial knowledge.

Then there are those who refuse to believe anything they do not see with their own eyes. They believe that truth is what you see and that it is unscientific to believe in things you cannot see. Like the *tampankan,* they fail to see the whole.

We see with our minds and hearts, not only with our eyes. If our minds are not focused on something, we do not see it. This is why it matters how we maintain our hearts and minds. We generally assume that our own view of things is normal. Yet people's perceptions can be surprisingly strange.

Things do not seem to be going the way we want them to because we are, as it were, looking at the world upside down. We have to acknowledge and accept this fact before we can even attempt to change a life that is not turning out the way we want into one that is more satisfying.

The Japanese observe the Bon Festival (the Festival of the Dead) between August 13 and 16. *Bon,* short for *urabon,* derives from the Sanskrit *ullambana,* meaning "hanging upside down." The Bon Festival is said to have originated in prayers for the dead, some of whom might be hanging upside down in a Buddhist hell. This same Sanskrit word may stem from the Persian word *urvan,* "soul." The ceremony, still followed in Iran, of burning wood to attract the souls of dead loved ones is very similar to the Japanese practice of lighting a small fire to welcome the ancestral spirits on the eve of the Bon Festival. The concept spread from Iran to India, to China, and to Japan.

Basically, *ullambana* describes the human tendency to perceive things upside down. In Buddhism this is how "perverted creatures" perceive—people who see things upside down rather than as they really are and assume that their judgment is always correct. Such people are annoyed by well-intentioned criticism or easily duped by gentle words of temptation, mistaking them for kindness. We are irritated by the speeding cars that menace us as we try to cross a street. Yet when *we* are driving, we are angered by the pedestrian taking his time to cross. In both cases, we see only from our own perspective and are blind to that of others.

Preconceptions Are Like Blinders

The Buddhist term *kuge* literally means "flowers of illusion," referring to the visionary existence produced by delusion. When our eyes are tired, we sometimes see spots and lines. They disappear when we blink but then come right back again. The spots and lines are not really there, but our tired eyes make us think they are. The illusions of our desires and appetites are like that: *kuge.*

Our illusions make us think "maybe," then "probably," then "certainly." Take someone who has worked hard for a company. He is convinced that he has played a major role in the company's growth. Yet one day he finds himself shunted to a dead-end job in the general affairs department. The company president seems to listen only to the opinions of the head of the sales department. The unhappy person in general affairs decides that the head of the sales department has said bad things about him and that is why he has been placed in such an unimportant position. He is so certain of it that he refuses even to consider that there might be other reasons for his demotion.

And what is really unfortunate is that he becomes incapable of any other point of view. Once we become obsessed with an idea, our vision narrows sharply. We forget that there may be other ways to interpret a situation. Like an insect in a spider's web, the more we struggle, the more we enmesh ourselves.

Seeing the whole picture is never more important than in a difficult situation. When we do this we can pinpoint the cause of our troubles and see where we went wrong. To put it another way, when we measure our thinking against the yardstick of the heavens, a great discrepancy becomes obvious. Recognizing this discrepancy is what enlightenment is all about.

Clear Reflections

Why do people not see clearly? The Buddha told a parable to illustrate how difficult clear-sightedness can be. One day one of his disciples said, "Sometimes my mind is crystal clear and I preach eloquently. At other times my mind is confused and I cannot think of what to say. Why is this?"

The Buddha replied, "See here a large vessel of water. If the water is tinted red or green, your face will not be accurately reflected in it. In the same way, when our hearts and minds are clouded by various defilements and desires, we cannot perceive anything as it really is. Now think what happens when this vessel is placed on a fire and the water begins to boil." The hot, bubbling water does not reflect anything. The angry mind is like boiling water. It becomes impossible for it to make rational judgments. The Buddha continued, "If bits of moss and grass fall into the water, it will no longer reflect things accurately. In the same way, when the heart and mind are polluted with folly and suspicion, they cannot reflect things as they truly are."

Well, then, you may ask, when does water reflect most accurately? When it is still and clear. The mountain lake, with its smooth, mirrorlike surface, reflects the mountain so accurately that the reflection looks exactly like the real thing. It is impossible to judge things reliably when our hearts and minds are clouded by desire or anger; we cannot think straight. No matter how good our eyesight may be, if we do not work hard to rid ourselves of suspicion and hatred, we will never be clear-sighted. And to be clear-sighted, we must always keep our hearts and minds tranquil and serene.

What Is Really Important

Move as if you mean to hit a dog with a stick and it will try to bite the stick. The dog directs its anger not at the human being wielding the stick but at the stick swinging toward it. If we are not careful, we are likely to make the same mistake.

There are, for example, people who criticize the Japanese flag as a symbol of military aggression. But obviously, no flag can wage war. What is really the problem is the spirit of militarism that forced the Japanese flag into China and Southeast Asia.

There is no need here to summarize the heated debate in Japan over the Japanese flag. I would like to point out, however, that international law prescribes respect for and protects the flag of every country. Our branches of Rissho Kosei-kai in the United States keep the Stars and Stripes in a place of honor and display it beside the altar as the sutras are recited. The American flag is respected as a symbol of the United States. Why should the Japanese flag not be given the same respect as the flags of other nations? How can we honor the flags of other nations if we cannot honor our own?

I remember reading a newspaper article about the 1993 visit of Japan's emperor and empress to Germany. One of the places they visited was the Japan-German Center in Berlin. It had been raining; a wet Japanese flag lay on the pavement, probably dropped by an enthusiastic well-wisher. The newspaper article described how the empress quietly stooped to pick it up. The incident was shown on German TV.

The debate over the flag is misdirected: the question is not whether it is a symbol of Japan's sins or a worthy emblem of Japan. We should shake off these obsessions and see the flag for what it really is: a patriotic symbol of our love for the country that nurtured us.

Learning from Our Mistakes

There are so many people who simply insist on seeing things upside down. Satan will use even the Bible, it is said, to achieve his own ends. Anything can be cast in a bad light if that is how we want to see it.

In 1987 more than nine hundred members of the People's Temple committed mass suicide in Guyana. In 1993 the Branch Davidians in Texas lost their church and ninety-five followers in the fire that started as the FBI moved in. In the eighteenth century, a church in czarist Russia took so seriously the biblical injunction to "cut off the hand or foot that offends thee" that the men in the congregation were forced to undergo castration. As the Chinese Buddhist classic *Tsung-ching-lu* says, "The water that the cow drinks becomes milk; the water that the viper drinks becomes poison."

The Buddhist sutras are said to contain as many as eighty-four thousand teachings. It would be easy to pick out only the one that served our purpose at any given time. The Bible, the

Buddhist sutras, and yes, even the Japanese flag all deserve reverence. What is really important, however, is how they are used. And this is where clear-sightedness comes in, for at the root of how we use things is how accurately we see what they really are. We cannot perceive the Japanese flag accurately, for example, without first delving into what drove Japan to militarism.

The German philosopher Immanuel Kant (1724–1804) claimed that war, not peace, is the natural human condition. Certainly, humanity has spent most of the past few centuries waging war. Even those brief periods in which there were no conflicts were merely times of preparation for war. Only a few hundred of the five thousand years of recorded history have been truly peaceful. The rest of the time people have been busy killing each other. We are still very clumsy at building peace. Some Japanese still argue over the Pacific war that ended more than fifty years ago. Some say it was a war of aggression, but others demur, pointing out that such a description hardly does justice to those brave soldiers who laid down their lives for the sake of country and family. War is never simple. What we need now is to learn from past mistakes. We should listen carefully to the anguished cries of all those who have lost their lives in war and heed their warnings for building for a better tomorrow. Surely that is the only way for us to console their souls and pray for their repose.

Many Rissho Kosei-kai youth think similarly and are working hard to help others, in such places as Kobe in the aftermath of the great earthquake of 1995, Nepal, Cambodia, the Philippines, Thailand, India, Africa, and the former Yugoslavia. In 1995 the Rissho Kosei-kai Fund for Peace supported forty-nine projects with roughly 600 million yen raised through the permanent Donate-a-Meal Movement, which began in 1975.

All the money was raised by Rissho Kosei-kai members, who solicited donations from others and skipped a few meals each month themselves, contributing the money they collected and saved to international assistance.

The reason we forgo a meal once in a while is not only to help the poor in developing countries but also to give ourselves the opportunity to reflect on our own prejudices and our excessively comfortable way of life. We receive much in return for such small acts of charity. Mother Teresa of Calcutta, who spent so many years caring for the destitute and the dying, said that a simple word of thanks whispered by a dying person gave her much, much more than she could ever give in return.

And so it is with our own acts of charity. Every time I see our young people working with steady devotion to help others, I give thanks that I have remained true to my faith. It especially heartens me to know that these young people are working of their own free will.

Chapter 9

The Power of Words

We all classify and judge the people and things around us on the basis of our own experience. But we are often obsessed with our assumptions, which can lead us to the wrong conclusions. Judging others by the most trivial characteristics and our self-imposed standards, we hastily decide whether we like people or dislike them. We rate them arbitrarily and are quick to calculate whether a relationship with them will be to our advantage or disadvantage.

For instance, Susie may praise someone for having sparkling eyes, good conversational ability, and being well dressed. Betty, on the other hand, may condemn the same person for being shifty eyed, talking too much, and wearing shoes that don't go with the rest of his outfit. No two people see things the same way; we each see the world through our own uniquely tinted glasses. And to further complicate matters, we are very unforgiving once we decide that we dislike someone or that he or she is bad. Suddenly, everything that person does is wrong.

"Right view" means a balanced outlook. Never forget that for every exterior there is an interior. You cannot judge fairly until you consider both. We should also keep in mind that we are prone to see only what we want to see, with complete disregard for the other person's feelings and thoughts.

The French mathematician, physicist, and philosopher Blaise Pascal (1623–1662) warned that before reprimanding or offering advice to someone, we should be careful to note that person's particular viewpoint. What may seem false to us may seem true to the other person. Look down at a cone from above and you see a circle; look at it from the side and you see a triangle. How foolish to argue over whether a cone is a circle or a triangle! Both views are true, depending on one's perspective.

One more condition for determining what is "correct" is to ensure that one's judgment can be accepted by all, in other words, that it reflects a viewpoint everyone can understand. Take this into account when you look at your circumstances and you will realize that the suffering and troubles you confront now are a golden opportunity to gain a whole new perspective on things. They are an opportunity to be reborn. Recognize this fact and your problems are half-solved.

To see things just as they are is to be objective. And to be objective, you must learn to rein in your self-centeredness. For example, parents will not always be able to manipulate their children. Every individual is irreplaceable and unique. No child can fulfill a parent's expectations 100 percent. If we accept that our children will someday leave our sides, we will be able to free ourselves of our parental desire to control and direct. We should understand that, at all times, what the child wants more than anything else is to be recognized and respected as an independent human being. If we accept and understand that truth, we will be able to think in the right way and do what parents should.

If "right thought" seems too vague, how about prudence?

If we are truly prudent, we will never be at a loss for "right speech," or the right words with which to encourage a child to become self-reliant and independent. Right speech strengthens the bonds between parent and child.

Right view, right thought, and right speech all refer to a way of living founded on the principles that all things are constantly changing and everything is interrelated.

Words That Move People

All kinds of words come to our lips every day. Words should link people, but if we are not careful, they can sever the ties between us. There is an old Jewish saying to the effect that "fish are always caught by the mouth; people too are caught by the mouth." Loose talk makes your world smaller and smaller. Soon no one believes anything you say.

Things depend a great deal on the way they are presented. Unpleasant truths will be accepted if told tactfully. Sincerity softens our words and makes them more palatable. We need to learn how to speak in a way that moves people. When we are sad, when we suffer, the simple words of someone who truly understands how we feel can lift us up and make us glad to be alive.

Words of praise are also important. Even the dourest person can be transformed by praise. The child who is regularly praised and reassured that she will certainly grow up into a fine adult, little by little makes those words come true. Words have a spirit of their own.

Ryokan, the Zen priest, poet, and calligrapher, said that all words should be spoken with feeling. The right words to make another person happy will not come to our lips unless we regularly endeavor to see only the good in others. What a joy it is to hear through a third party that we have been praised by someone we really care about! Zen master Dogen says in his *Shobogenzo* (Treasury of the Eye of the True Dharma) that we are happy to be praised to our faces, but that indirect words of praise will be etched deeply into our hearts. He lived more than 750 years ago, yet he could be instructing a management seminar today, so wise and apt are his perceptions.

Although it is fine to praise people in their absence, we must never criticize them behind their backs.

Reprimand Yourself When You Reprimand Others

Today Japanese women are playing an increasingly vital role in society and are active in many fields. A veteran corporate department head says that with more and more women in the workplace, the old rules no longer apply. "If you think they bow and scrape to me just because I'm the department head, you're wrong!" he declared.

Apparently, considerable sensitivity is required in the new workplace. For example, suppose the department head happens to be engaged in conversation and fails to respond immediately to a woman worker's "Good morning." She may be discouraged by this, complaining that she has been ignored. At the same time, the department head has found that a simple word of encouragement, a sign of concern, can do wonders to perk up his female staff. Traditional practices aside, I believe that male workers are just as sensitive and can be just as effectively encouraged by a boss who lets them know he cares. It is just that men have been trained to hide their feelings.

Anger and a reprimand are two different things. The Chinese character for *reprimand* is written with the symbol for "mouth" and that for "enlightenment" or "education." The character for *anger,* on the other hand, implies exposed emotions. We reprimand people in the hope of educating them; we get angry, however, only to vent our own harsh feelings.

In a book I mentioned earlier, *Mittsu Home, Futatsu Shikaru Jinzai Ikusei* (Praise Thrice and Scold Twice to Foster Someone's Potential), Sakio Sakagawa points out that when we admonish someone, we should keep in mind that every circumstance in which a reprimand becomes necessary is a reflection of our own minds and hearts. The one who does the chiding is just as much to blame for these circumstances as the one who receives the reprimand. Every boss who really wants to be understood by employees should approach them in that way.

We should be humble enough to acknowledge that if we were in the same position we might just as likely have erred as the person we are reprimanding. Those who are convinced that they would never err in such a way simply have never had to confront the same kind of situation. Reprimanding with compassion, which is the only right way, is possible only when we can say to ourselves, "Had it been me, I might have done the same thing." The founder of the Jodo Shin sect of Japanese Buddhism, Shinran (1173–1262), was recorded as saying in the *Tannisho* (Notes Lamenting Deviations) that anyone can occasionally do something out of character under certain circumstances. The most effective leader thoroughly understands and accepts this fact.

The Source of Human Misery

So far I have placed considerable stress on the two Buddhist principles of transience and selflessness: "all things are impermanent" and "nothing has an ego." Yet simple as these truths are, it is no easy task to apply them in our daily lives. Many people claim to understand them but are full of self-assertion and arrogance, or never stop complaining about incidents of long ago. They lead miserable lives, never knowing the joy of a life that is sustained by everything around them.

In Buddhism, the source of that misery is referred to as the Three Poisons. The first is covetousness or sensual desire, an appetite so powerful it can never be satisfied. It is far from the aspiration to self-improvement. Covetousness is the first of the Three Poisons because unbridled desire always leads to suffering. The Buddha by no means condemned desire; the important thing is to rein it in.

The second poison is anger or ill will. This is not the kind of anger that is quick to flare but just as quickly dies down. It is the kind that simmers, like a deep grudge. "Grab another person's torch with the wind against you and you will be burned," warns the Chinese sutra *Chu-yao-ching*. Allow your anger to take control and you will only wear yourself down. Anger can be as immobilizing as any disease and as thoroughly self-consuming as a fierce flame. The Buddha admonishes us in the Sutra of the Great Accumulation of Treasures that anger destroys in an instant the "good roots" of virtue that we have painstakingly accumulated over a long time. Only forbearance can subdue anger. We must have fortitude to withstand the enemy within ourselves, our own anger, just as we must defend ourselves from enemies that attack us from without.

The third poison is foolishness or ignorance. You cannot see clearly or judge correctly if you are always complaining about what cannot be helped. Buddhism teaches that only by extinguishing the fire lit by the Three Poisons can we cross to the other shore of peace and rest.

Reaching the Other Shore

By the other shore, I mean nirvana, the realm of the ideal. I am not referring to the world after death. The *Dhammapada* (verse 85) says,

> Few among many are those who reach the other shore [of enlightenment],
> While most run up and down along this side of the river.

This shore is the world of our daily lives, a world in which we are possessed by our desires (covetousness), in which we fight over petty issues (anger or ill will), and in which we are constantly complaining of things' being unfair (foolishness or delusion). We must rid ourselves of the filth of our desires before we can even hope to attain the other shore.

The *Dhammapada* (verse 369) also says, "O *bhikshus* [monks], empty the boat that is your life; once emptied it will quickly glide. When you remove the passions and dangerous desires you will be on the way to nirvana." A boat filled with water will not make much headway. In the same way, if we load our hearts and minds with too many burdens, we will never be able to move forward. Before doing anything else, we must first get rid of the unneeded water. Lightened of its load, our boat will sail swiftly to the other shore. Each of us must accomplish this in his or her own way.

Buddhism teaches that we reap what we sow. Most often this statement is interpreted negatively: an evil deed will bring only equal evil in return. It also has a positive meaning, however. Much good can be obtained if we work hard at doing good deeds. Through this teaching, Buddhism is trying to show that, regardless of whether they are good or evil, we must always take responsibility for our own words and deeds.

The Records of Master Lin-chi, a compilation of teachings of Lin-chi (Rinzai), the founder of the sect of Ch'an (Zen) Buddhism that bears his name, says that if you are the master of yourself, wherever you are, the truth will predominate in whatever place you occupy. The person who lacks self-mastery will constantly complain that everything is someone else's fault. "This happened because so-and-so said that." "I objected, but everyone insisted on going ahead." Such people can never admit that they might have been wrong.

Our mistakes invariably arise from our lack of self-assurance and our tendency to allow others to dictate what we think and do.

The Virtue of Pliability

When I was only sixteen I left my hometown of Tokamachi in the mountains of Niigata Prefecture and found a job in Tokyo. Yet even then I never thought of myself as a hired hand doing only as I was told. I always had ideas and never hesitated to offer suggestions to the boss. "Wouldn't this be a better way?" I would suggest. My boss would reply, "Maybe so. Go ahead and give it a try." Sometimes we forgot who was the employer and who was the employee. I was the master of my own circumstances.

My boss's wife used to praise me, saying, "Mr. Niwano is so diligent. He is square yet pliant, like a block of tofu." I always thought that was a good analogy. Only recently did I discover, in Shigeta Saito's book *Tofu no Gotoku* (Like Tofu), that the analogy was first used by the haiku poet Seisensui Ogiwara

(1884–1976). In a passage headed "Tofu," Ogiwara describes a good man:

> He is soft and pliant and yet firm enough that he does not
>   disintegrate.
> He can be boiled or roasted and tastes good either way.
> He adapts naturally to all circumstances without complaint.

> I aspire to the firm pliability of a block of tofu.

Chapter 10

Achieving Our Hidden Potential

In chapter 4 I mentioned the garment into which the whole universe has been woven. Would you be surprised if I told you that in the same way, our whole being is imbued with the universe, encompassing a distant past we cannot remember and a distant future we cannot imagine? Most of the time, of course, we do not think about this; we do not even conceive of the possibility.

The famous mathematician Kiyoshi Oka once said, "Human beings are indeed strange and contradictory. You cannot really satisfy or convince a person with only knowledge, logic, reasoning, or rules and regulations. And the person who is not fully convinced is not going to act with conviction. It is a person's emotions that we really have to speak to and convince."

We tend to assume that people are motivated by personal gain, but Dr. Oka pointed out that that is not everything. People's feelings and emotions are what is most important. Even the simplest likes and dislikes arise out of complex feelings that cannot be explained by logic alone. Whether or not we like a person does not depend solely on advantage or disadvantage, beauty or ugliness. Part of us makes the judgment before our reasoning mind has a chance to evaluate such factors. This process happens beyond the control of our will.

"She is attractive and very likable. She also has a gentle disposition. She's almost too good for you," people may say to a young man, yet somehow he just may not be attracted to her. On the other hand, the woman who is criticized for being bossy may be just the person for him. There is no telling whom we are going to like or dislike.

Our feelings arise from the most profound depths of our hearts and minds, where all the thoughts and feelings of past experience that we forgot long ago are accumulated, tangled up together. Our feelings—our habits of thought and emotion—are the products of this accumulation. Our feelings control and move us without our conscious will. The whole of our past is like a tree that bears the fruit of our present emotions and makes us what we are. Our every word and action is prompted by this internal unconscious world. We speak of "inadvertently" saying or doing something. What we do not realize is that we are being prompted by the feelings and thoughts deep down at the bottom of our hearts and minds. It is these unconscious feelings and thoughts that dictate our individual character, our behavior, and even the boundaries of our capabilities.

Unknown Memories within the Brain

In our brains is an information checkpoint called the thalamus. All signals to the brain must pass through the thalamus before being processed by the frontal lobe. These signals come from both inside and outside ourselves. Our internal signals originate in a mass of forgotten information tens of thousands of times greater than the information of which we are consciously aware. We have no memory of this information, yet it remains within us, locked deep within our cells. All this forgotten information would create havoc if it were allowed to spill into the conscious mind. The thalamus acts as a safety valve to prevent such leakage.

It is possible, I have learned, to open that safety valve with ascetic practice, such as fasting. A television program aired by Japan Broadcasting Corporation explained how this opening works. The vast store of our unconscious memory includes all of our experiences, without judgment of their significance—from the forgotten events of childhood to the experiences common to all humankind without regard to race, culture, or time. The whole of this memory is too vast for today's science to explain. I believe that if we could only see this totality, we would realize that our individual existence is but an extension of life continuing from the remote past. We would also be able to see, I believe, that our own existence is intimately interconnected with all of humanity in a dimension that we cannot even conceive with our conscious minds.

A Storehouse of Unconscious Memory

In his search for the means of release from human suffering, Shakyamuni tried a variety of ascetic practices. He sat for hours in meditation and stopped breathing. He fasted, eating only one grain of rice and one berry or nut each day. He fasted until he had become a mere skeleton, his ribs protruding through his skin. For six long years he tortured his body in this way, to the point, as legend has it, that moss grew on him.

At Rissho Kosei-kai, we once practiced the training method of cold ablutions, in which one wakes up before dawn to pour several buckets of cold water over one's head. In my youth I did that every morning and evening for two whole years. I would rise at three in the morning and go outside the house where a big barrel of water stood. There I would pour buckets of water over myself. In the winter I had to break the ice that formed on top of the water in the barrel. My neighbors later told me jokingly that just hearing my splashing early every morning had made them shiver in their warm beds. Supposedly one can develop a knack for doing this practice, but the shock of the ice-cold water always gave me a headache.

Shakyamuni underwent much more rigorous training; yet though he brought himself to the brink of death, he did not find enlightenment. Concluding that no amount of self-torture would bring enlightenment, the Buddha bathed in a nearby river and ate the milk gruel brought to him by a village maiden. He then sat in meditation under the Bodhi tree. Only then was he able to achieve supreme enlightenment.

I like to think that Shakyamuni was enlightened to the truth of this world—that, in terms of time, all life has been interconnected since the remotest past and, in terms of space, everything that exists is connected with everything else. People and things, even their surroundings, are born, die, and change in accordance with the law of dependent origination. This is the starting point of all the Buddha's teachings.

In the unconscious world, in the depths of our hearts and minds, are recorded all the things that we have seen, heard, and experienced as children. Yet these are not all just individual experiences; even the experiences shared by the entire human race are recorded there. This unconscious world is affecting us in the deepest recesses of our hearts.

This unconscious world can be found and explored through

the practice of yoga. The workings of the unconscious mind, in somewhat difficult Buddhist terminology, can be described with the phrase "the seeds produce manifestations," which means "everything is manifested in the place of the consciousness only"—that is, the root of all our thoughts and actions is within the unconscious mind. Whom and what we like and dislike are dictated by feelings we cannot readily explain. In the most typical Buddhist view of the mind's structure, the doctrine of the Consciousness-Only school, the source of these feelings is called *mano*-consciousness. Its effects are stored in an even deeper consciousness known as *alaya*-consciousness. When conditions are ripe, these accumulated effects emerge as our present actions.

If we effectively tap this storehouse of effects, we can make our own the experiences and wisdom of the infinite past. The human mind and soul hold immeasurable power, which can be used for good or evil. In the wrong circumstances, for example, the doctor whose mission should be to save lives can become an instrument of death. On one hand, we have this wonderful hidden potential. On the other, we are fettered by the ties of the conscious mind so that often we cannot exert proper control over our actions.

Purifying Our Innermost Minds

In Japanese, the Buddhist term for ignorance, *mumyo,* is written with the characters for "no light." It is this lack of light, or ignorance, that gives birth to all defilements and confusion. The light of wisdom does not penetrate the darkness of the ignorant soul. If we eliminate ignorance, we eliminate life's suffering at the same time.

We may know that doing a particular thing is good, but this does not always mean that we are able to act on it immediately. All too often we make only the most feeble attempt to do good. Similarly, we may know that doing a certain thing is bad, yet we cannot stop ourselves. This is *mumyo*. Consider the person who just cannot seem to respond with a simple "yes" when someone calls. Why is it so difficult to respond? Because the self wants to interfere in everything.

People are more apt to be controlled by feelings than by reason. The question is how to open up the world of the unconscious that is the source of these feelings. The key to tapping the power of the unconscious mind is making an effort to turn our conscious minds toward wisdom and doing good.

When a Ch'an (Zen) master of great virtue named Niao-k'e, who used to practice meditation in a tree, was asked by the T'ang poet Po Chü-i what the essence of Buddhism was, he replied, "Doing no evil, doing all that is good, and purifying your mind. This is the teaching of all the buddhas." By "purifying your mind" I am sure he meant that we must purify our deepest unconscious self as well. The only way to do that is to avoid all evil and do much good. Only in this way can we gradually rid ourselves of self-centeredness and purify the innermost recesses of the soul.

Only Action Leads to Achievement

When I was in elementary school, each morning our principal posted a maxim and made all the students recite it in loud voices. One of his favorite sayings was: "If you try, you can do it. If you do not try, you cannot do it. In everything you do, if you say you cannot do it, that means you have not yet tried."

So said Uesugi Yozan (1751–1822), a *daimyo* (feudal lord) who restored the fortunes of the impoverished Yonezawa domain. I read those words every morning without much thought, but now I realize how important they are. Nothing will happen if you do not try to do something. You cannot achieve a goal if you are not determined to act for it. You should apply yourself to the point where you are free from concern about gain and loss. Become a great fool, and inevitably others will appear who will go forward with you. The first step is to tell yourself, "All right, I'm really going to do this and do it right." Simple determination is a wonderful source of energy. I have never been as certain of that as I am now. The second step is to act with a prayerful heart.

Most people apply themselves to a degree but can never seem really to throw themselves into their work. The Japanese word for "mindfulness" or "intention" is written with the two characters for "now" and "heart." In other words, we must put our whole hearts now into what we wish to achieve. We will not get very far if we are distracted by doubts. Our instinct is to protect ourselves from failure. We hesitate to give our all because we are terrified of making a mistake. We allow our doubts to kill our power to act.

At every corporate meeting there is someone who objects to any innovative idea. "What if it does not work?" she asks. Yoshio Hatakeyama, chairman of the Japan Efficiency Association and author of a book on good management, gives the following advice:

> Once you decide on doing something, stop using words like *cannot, impossible,* and *difficult.* If your subordinates use them, you will know that they are trying to tell you one

of three things: this cannot be done with the methods we have been using so far; it is impossible to do this right now; or this is too difficult for me to do alone. Once you interpret their words in this way, it becomes easier to figure a way to get around their objections.

If something cannot be done with the methods used so far, look for a new approach. If it is impossible to do right now because of a lack of the people and funds needed, think about what can be done with the people and funds available. You might only achieve five to ten percent of your goal at first. That's fine; it is a start. Think about how to achieve fifteen percent the next year and thirty percent the year after. And if your aim cannot be achieved alone, find others to help you.

As I have already pointed out, the only way to achieve anything is to convince yourself you can do it and then go ahead and do it. Are you better today than you were yesterday? How do you compare yourself this year with the way you were last year? Only by constantly looking back in this way can we move forward.

Everyone has some kind of talent or special trait. There is no shame in not being able to do something another person excels in. More important is how much progress we have made compared with our own past selves. To live with hope is to live with faith. We must live each day with an ideal goal in mind.

In my childhood my grandfather used to tell me, "Even insects do what they need to do to feed themselves. You must grow up to become a person who strives for a better world, who acts to benefit others." He repeated these words so often that they became engraved on my heart. Somewhere along the way I have come to live by them. As a small child, I had no idea what it meant to strive for a better world and live for others, yet now these words are my driving force.

Listening with Humility

In training, constant repetition is important. The outcome of a sumo match, it is said, is already determined when the wrestlers first square off. Set yourself in the right position and you will be able to move smoothly without hesitation. Your opponent will not have a chance. But getting into the right position is not something you can do right away; it takes practice, practice, practice.

For a sumo wrestler, training begins right after junior high school. He wakes up every morning in the predawn darkness and practices and practices until he is exhausted and covered with dirt. This he does every day, year after year. It will take years before he achieves just the right stance—before, as the Japanese say, "he discovers his own, personal kind of sumo."

Taiho was one of the greatest sumo grand champions of all time. During the early 1960s, he and Kashiwado set the pace of all sumo for years to come. Kashiwado's winning technique was to leap forward and grab his opponent's bellyband or belt and force him out of the ring, all in an instant. Taiho, on the other hand, had a naturally flexible style that allowed him to adapt to and defeat even the toughest opponents. His kind of sumo led him to thirty-two tournament victories.

Taiho's power lay in his humility. When his stablemaster advised him on how he should approach an opponent, he did exactly as he was told. I mentioned this characteristic of Taiho's to the famous Kabuki actor Nizaemon Kataoka XIII one day and he clapped his hands in agreement. "How true!" he said, "When I get a pupil who really listens to what I say, I find myself giving him all kinds of advice. A sincere willingness to pay attention makes all the difference."

The average sumo wrestler forgets his master's advice as soon as he is facing an opponent. Once in the ring, he uses the moves that he is best at, and because he is not reading the opponent properly, he loses. But Taiho paid attention to his master's guidance and always did exactly as he was told. He listened with humility; that was what made him one of the greatest grand champions in sumo history.

Sticking to the Straight Path

Financial speculation was rife in Japan during the economic bubble of the 1980s. The Japanese dictionary defines *toki,* meaning "speculation," as acting to achieve something that is uncertain but that will lead to much profit if successful. The Japanese word comes from a Buddhist term meaning "the state in which the hearts and minds of master and disciple are one."

The Japanese word for management, *keiei,* is another term originating in Buddhism. It used to mean the diligence involved in applying oneself to the achievement of a set goal. The character for *kei* is the same as that used for *kyo,* meaning "sutra." It derives from the Sanskrit word for "thread." In the corporate world, profit is achieved only when management follows a single thread of logic. Managers must have a driving idea, a single conviction, if they are to be effective. Beads, though they may have different colors and shapes, still make an effective rosary if strung on the same thread. The successful corporation is one in which management and employees are joined together (*toki*) on the same thread of conviction.

I have heard that the English word *company* originally

referred to a group of people sharing a loaf of bread. Japanese has a similar concept that refers to friends who have eaten rice out of the same pot. This reminds me of a little story that very effectively illustrates the importance of sticking to a single thread of conviction.

Three men were piling up stones. A passerby stopped and asked what they were doing.

The first man replied, "We were told to pile these stones, so that is what we are doing."

The second man said, "I am piling up these stones to make a wall." Unlike the first man's response, this one clearly indicated a goal.

Finally, the third man said, "I am building a church."

This last man not only knows exactly what he is trying to achieve, but also takes pride in his purpose. This story is told in many forms. Sometimes the last man is building a castle; at other times it is a pyramid. The main point is that the last man knows exactly what he is aiming for and what his particular function is to achieve that objective. Such knowledge and conviction make for good management.

Buddhism points out the folly of pursuing profits that will disappear like soap bubbles. Great merchant households like Mitsui and Mitsubishi have survived to this day because their founders pursued their aims with a firm philosophy that served as a set of "family precepts." The Mitsuis, for example, were originally wine merchants who later became money changers and then kimono merchants. The Mitsui mottoes have much to teach us even today: "Greed breeds discontent. Everything has its limit." "The children of the family must start at the bottom." "If someone in the family strays, a family council should be held and immediate action taken."

As one successful businessman has said, "I judge people by their consistency. I do not have much to do with people whose opinions change every time I meet them." We judge a person's value by the strength and consistency of her innermost being.

Chapter 11

Motivated by Our Hidden Self

The term *depth psychology* brings to mind images of Sigmund Freud (1856–1939) and Carl Jung (1875–1961). Freud began his psychoanalytic practice with the treatment of hysteria at a time when this neurosis was not yet a recognized disease. It is said that his involvement in depth psychology research was motivated by the results of his concurrent experiments with hypnosis.

A hypnotized person will act as directed. "When I give the signal, go to the window and look outside," says the hypnotist, and that is exactly what the hypnotized person does. Yet when awakened from the hypnotized state, the person has no memory of what he did. Seeing how people could be manipulated in this way, Freud reasoned that hidden in the human mind was a vast unknown world, which he dubbed "the unconscious." Might not the origins of human actions be found here, he wondered, in the depths of the unconscious mind? Freud's discovery opened the way to a whole new field of human psychology.

Freud was a man of the nineteenth century, but people in

India had been studying the unconscious mind long before his time. The Consciousness-Only doctrine of the Yogacara school of Mahayana Buddhism, formulated in the fifth century, emphasized the human mind and heart and examined the structure and function of the mind's unknown regions. This doctrine was amply interpreted and commented on over the centuries, thus becoming an important part of contemporary Buddhism.

In brief, the Consciousness-Only doctrine states that the human being maintains contact with the external world through the six sense organs: the eyes, ears, nose, tongue, body, and mind. We see with our eyes, hear with our ears, smell with our nose, taste with our tongue, and touch with our body—and then process it all with our mind. We have a wonderful "multimedia" existence, applying our whole being, for example, to judging which river is likely to have the most fish and which forest should be avoided because of its bears.

We see a puppy and think with our mind, "What a cute puppy!" We listen to music and think with our mind, "What a pretty tune!" We tend to assume that this mind of ours represents our soul, but the mind influenced by the senses is only a superficial consciousness. Deeper, much deeper, is the *mano*-consciousness, and even further down, the *alaya*-consciousness. The *mano*-consciousness is completely self-centered. It is what we often refer to as our selfish desires and ego and is therefore tainted. It is our *mano*-consciousness that decides what we like and dislike, what we think is beautiful and what we think is ugly. The impressions formulated in the *mano*-consciousness are stored in the recesses of the *alaya*-consciousness. The *alaya*-consciousness is the repository of all of our experiences since birth. Also located there are the memories of past lives, stored very much like seeds to be planted later. A seed contains within itself its infinite past as well as the potential for an infinite future; thus, the *alaya*-consciousness is also referred to as the "storehouse-consciousness." This part of the mind is like a seed, which seems lifeless because it does not move. Yet it sprouts into life under the proper temperature and humidity.

Hidden beneath the Soiled Surface

The *alaya*-consciousness is the most important part of the inner, deep mind. It is believed to share the same characteristics as the Tathagata and is sometimes referred to as the buddha-nature. In the *alaya*-consciousness, in other words, is our potential to attain buddhahood.

While some say that the *alaya*-consciousness is one and the same as the buddha-nature, others insist that deep within the *alaya*-consciousness is yet another level of undefiled consciousness called the *amala*-consciousness. It is here, the proponents of this theory claim, that we find the pure internal being that is free of all delusions and filth. This theory was promoted by, among others, Paramartha, the eminent sixth-century translator of scriptures; it diverges from mainstream Buddhist thinking. Indeed, since the *alaya*-consciousness contains both good seeds and bad seeds, it is also called the "union-of-truth-and-illusion consciousness."

The feelings and thoughts that we assume originate in our minds and hearts are actually the products of the most superficial layer of our consciousness. We apologize "from the bottom of our heart" and vow never to repeat our errors, yet it is not long before we find ourselves doing the same things again. This is because our feeling of remorse is only superficial, not really from the bottom of our heart at all.

This discussion has become quite esoteric. The point I

am trying to make is that, however clouded and murky our thoughts and feelings may seem, we all bear deep within us the buddha-nature. The core of Buddhist teaching consists of awakening us to the presence of this buddha-nature within ourselves. The buddha-nature is not a physical organ that we can point to. It is an intangible essence that enables us to follow the Way of the bodhisattva and which grows in brilliance with every step we take on this Way.

In Sanskrit, the buddha-nature is called the *tathagata-garbha*. *Tathagata* refers to the Buddha. *Garbha* is an embryo. Every person bears the embryo of the Tathagata; it is no exaggeration to say that the aim of Buddhism is to help each individual give birth to this inner being. Unfortunately, our buddha-nature is enveloped in the mantle of our self-centered desires. Remove (*dis-*) this mantle (*cover*) and we will "discover" our own buddha-nature.

Our superficial consciousness does endeavor to do good, but because the motivation does not come from the deeper *alaya*-consciousness, we find it hard to stick to our good intentions and are easily overtaken by selfish thoughts and desires. Human goodness is necessarily limited in scope. We know in our conscious mind that something is good, but we find it difficult to act for this goodness. Even when we do perform good deeds, we cannot keep it up for very long because of the constant battle between the good and bad natures within ourselves.

We need to draw upon the deep reserve of purity hidden in the *alaya*-consciousness if we are to successfully control both our *mano*-consciousness and our superficial consciousness. The various practices of Buddhism, such as Zen, cleanse both types of consciousness. All Buddhist practice aims to help us discover and awaken to our own inner buddha-nature.

Knowing Our Own Failings

In India, the right hand is considered clean and the left unclean. Placing the clean hand against the unclean one creates the pose of prayer, a pose by which we acknowledge our unclean natures even as we aspire to divine purity. We create a pose that says, "Please help me; I am very much in the dark." Nothing, I think, so clearly reveals the human condition.

In chapter 3 of the Lotus Sutra, "A Parable," the Buddha says,

> Now this triple world
> All is my domain;
> The living beings in it
> All are my children.

You might say that we all share the same genes as the Buddha. Regrettably, most people live out their lives without ever realizing their buddha-natures. What a waste to leave our greatest treasure hidden in the depths of our *alaya*-consciousness!

Something has long bothered me. When news of a plane crash with no survivors is reported by the mass media, we feel a moment of sadness. Yet when the newscaster continues, "None of the passengers appears to have been Japanese," we let out a sigh of relief. Our feelings of sorrow are quick to dissipate the moment we realize that the accident has no personal connection with us, not even a remote one. Thus does our superficial consciousness limit the scope of goodness. We will never transcend this limitation as long as we live solely by our superficial consciousness. And the only way to overcome its confines is to strive for the benefit of others, not just for ourselves. This effort involves the pursuit of the bodhisattva practice, which is available to us precisely because of our inherent buddha-nature.

At first, our motivation may be partly selfish, but as we continue to apply ourselves to working for the benefit of others, our buddha-nature begins to shine forth. In time, we learn to savor the kind of deep joy and thanksgiving that can come only from true, selfless giving.

Socrates spoke of the midwifery of the mind. Buddhist practice ultimately does the same thing, assisting, as it were, in the birth of the buddha-nature within us. In this sense, all Buddhist education can be perceived as the art of midwifery.

Discrimination Leads to Conflict

Life is full of conflict. Individuals fight and countries fight, each side convinced that it is right and the other wrong. But no matter how loudly we assert ourselves, there can be no real justice or peace without the manifestation of the buddha-nature that resides within each and every one of us. Hatred and conflict will never cease as long as the true self remains hidden.

The Bible says, "Let him who is without sin cast the first stone." There can never be peace until we acknowledge our own failings. I think I can safely say that all religions teach us to look into ourselves and recognize our own drawbacks and imperfections. This is no easy thing to do and is an issue we will grapple with for all time.

The Sutra of Innumerable Meanings says, "All living beings discriminate falsely: 'It is this' or 'It is that,' and 'It is advantageous' or 'It is disadvantageous'; they entertain evil thoughts, make various karmas, and [thus] transmigrate within the six realms of existence; and they suffer all manner of miseries." Because of our tendency to be self-centered and to judge

everything and everyone in terms of how they relate to ourselves, we always seek to make evaluations of good and bad.
But this kind of discrimination is the source of all kinds of
human conflict.

A recent trend I find especially troubling is the increase in
divorces among couples married for thirty-five years or more.
This phenomenon would not need to exist if we were a little
less self-righteous and more willing to concede that we might
be at fault.

Taking One Small Step Aside

A Zen maxim states that even though you may be constantly
stepping aside on a narrow path to allow others to pass by,
within a whole lifetime you will have given way only one hundred times. Pride demands that we stand firm and not give way
to others. But when you are walking along a narrow path, you
will bump into people coming from the other direction unless
you step aside to let them pass. One small step can prevent
violent confrontation. Within your lifetime you will probably
have to give way like this a mere one hundred times or fewer.

How foolish we are to willingly enter confrontations that
may sometimes even escalate into court cases, all because we
refuse to take that one small step aside. Stepping aside, opening the way for others, is to acknowledge and worship the
buddha-nature in other people. This kind of action polishes
our own buddha-nature, making it glow even brighter than
before.

I visited China for the first time when that great country was
just opening up to the world after the chaos of Mao Zedong's
Cultural Revolution. There was much criticism of General
Lin Biao, formerly Mao's handpicked successor and now

condemned as a traitor, and of Confucius, whose teachings Lin Biao had interpreted to his own advantage. Prior to my departure from Japan a foreign ministry official warned me, "Whatever you do, don't talk about Confucius!"

Above all else, Confucius stressed good manners. The discourteous person, Confucius warned, would not survive in society. The Chinese of Mao's day claimed that this kind of thinking served only to support the elite and was not fitting in a truly egalitarian society. I was convinced, however, that two thousand years of Confucian teaching could not be erased by a brief uprising like the Cultural Revolution. Surely, I thought, Confucian wisdom could still be found deep in the hearts and minds of the Chinese people.

But when I went to China I found that some people were eager to denounce the wisdom of the past. Our interpreter-guide was quite rigid; when a conversation on how good walking was for the health happened to touch upon golf, he launched into a long speech: "Golf is a bourgeois sport not for the masses." Yet less than a decade later all the turmoil of the Cultural Revolution had died down. I even heard that a golf course had been built just outside Beijing. Today there is renewed respect for Confucius's teachings.

At the core of Confucianism is the principle of benevolence, or *jin,* a compound word written with the Chinese characters for "person" and "two." Benevolence, in other words, is the generosity and tolerance between two people that makes good relations possible. In Chinese, *human being* was originally written with the characters for "human" and "interval" or "space." Humans, in other words, exist in relationship to each other; we live together, not alone. The person without affection cannot be said to be living humanely—or even humanly.

The Buddha's Heart in a Devil's Child

The title *the Buddha* means "enlightened one"; it was conferred on Shakyamuni when he awakened to the truth. Mahayana Buddhism teaches that enlightenment is the awakening of the buddha-nature found in every individual. We all have the potential to become buddhas.

Skeptics doubt this idea. But a story told by Shigeru Kurashina aptly illustrates this belief. Kurashina has worked with juvenile delinquents for nearly forty years and was at one time director of the Matsumoto Reformatory in Nagano Prefecture. The boys and girls Kurashina encountered in his work had done things much worse than striking a teacher or shoplifting; many had ties with gangster organizations. In his effort to find ways to reform these children, Kurashina tried to learn as much as he could about psychology, education, and psychoanalysis, but nothing seemed to work. Only in the last ten years or so, he says, did he come to realize that he should be relating to his charges as fellow human beings instead of being preoccupied with how to handle them. When he began to recognize this truth, the words of a predecessor finally came home to him: "Far back in the heart of every child resides the divine. Treat each child with the same respect and reverence you would show to the divine."

Another story, familiar to most Americans, illustrates the same principle. It is the story of an eight-year-old girl living in New York City many years ago, who wrote this letter to the *New York Sun:*

Dear Editor,
I am 8 years old. Some of my little friends say there is no

Santa Claus. Papa says, "If you see it in the *Sun,* it's so."
Please tell me the truth, is there a Santa Claus?

Virginia O'Hanlon

The paper rallied to the call and replied in what has become
one of the most famous editorials of all time. Here is the cen-
tral portion of it:

Yes, Virginia, there is a Santa Claus. He exists as certainly
as love and generosity and devotion exist, and you know
that they abound and give to your life its highest beauty and
joy. Alas! How dreary would be the world if there were no
Santa Claus! It would be as dreary as if there were no Virgi-
nias. There would be no childlike faith then, no poetry, no
romance to make tolerable this existence. We should have
no enjoyment, except in sense and sight.

The most real things in the world are those that neither children nor adult can see.

It is true that the most important things cannot be seen.
And we adults must teach this fact to our children. To return
to Kurashina's story, over his nearly forty years of reformatory
work he dealt with more than forty thousand boys and girls.
Not one of these youngsters had shown any sign of religious
feeling or reverence for the gods and buddhas. "Their parents
probably never taught them any religious principles," Kurashina says. The responsibility for the lack of ethical and religious training, he goes on to assert, rests solely with the family.
Of course, just because a child observes a parent in the pose
of prayer at the family's Buddhist altar does not mean that the
child will become religious. But no child will even attempt to
enter the religious world without a parent's guidance.

Chapter 12

Every Life Needs Goals

Just as the planet Earth and each of the other planets must move in its own predetermined orbit, so human beings must abide by certain rules and principles. By keeping these principles, we ensure our own freedom. In other words, freedom requires self-control. Without standards by which to measure things, our societies could never function with any semblance of order.

Offer people an ambitious goal that will most certainly be difficult to achieve and they will wave you away: "You are being too idealistic." Yet it is precisely because we have ideals to strive for that we can make progress. When we have ideals, we can measure ourselves against them and see where we are lacking. In Buddhism this progression toward an ideal is referred to as *shojin* (effort), or the constant striving for perfection.

We cannot yet journey to the stars, but we can navigate the dark oceans of night thanks to the stars' brilliance. We all need a compass to guide us in this world; that is why I think it is so important to venerate the Buddha, who shows us the model of the ideal human being.

The more we learn about this ideal, the more we realize how immature we are and how far we have to go. This realization can be humbling. Without such a high standard, however, we would be quick to assume that we had perfected ourselves and therefore could do no wrong when pushing our ideas through. "The fool who recognizes his own foolishness is wise. The fool who believes himself wise is a true fool," says the *Dhammapada*. Human growth, I believe, requires that we never forget our own shortcomings and that we always be straightforward and honest.

Mahayana Buddhism places more importance on the process by which we strive for a goal than on attainment of the goal itself. The French writer André Gide (1869–1951) pointed out how extraordinary it can be to continue doing the same ordinary things in the same ordinary way, day in and day out. To do the same things every day without tiring of the routine, to repeat even one thing over and over every day: the point is that we should concentrate on improving the things and situations with which we come into contact instead of always seeking better things and better conditions.

Concentrate on the here and now. Think of your present job, for example, as something you have been fated to do. Treasure what you have and you will find peace of mind. The German economist Max Weber (1864–1920) referred to work as a vocation, a calling from God. The Shinto religion also refers to work as an office or mission that the gods have entrusted to a person. It does not matter what our work is. What is important is that we strive, through our work, to be of service to others.

A Pleasant Boulevard with a Satisfying View

So many things in this world cannot be clearly defined as either black or white. In fact, most things exist in a vague world of gray. The baseball umpire, for example, does not always know for certain whether a pitched ball that flew by at 140 kilometers per hour was a strike or a ball. Yet he can never say, "I'm just not sure." The same applies to the *gyoji* who referees a sumo match. When both wrestlers tumble out of the ring simultaneously, he still has to decide who is the winner; he cannot simply say, "I don't know."

Yet even though it is widely acknowledged that the human ability to make such judgments has a limit, the baseball umpire's word is final. And when there is a question about the *gyoji*'s decision in sumo, the judges sitting around the ring help him reach the correct one. In our daily lives, however, there is no one to guarantee that we will make the right decisions.

The English word *crossroads* refers to a place where one road intersects another. Every time we come to such a crossroads, we must decide which path to take. Our ability to choose correctly is vitally important in times of crisis. When we stand at a crossroads, we invariably are tempted to take the easier route, the way that promises to profit us most. I have always told myself, however, that I will never go wrong if I choose the way that seems most difficult. The easy downhill trek is always followed by a long and tedious climb. One might as well tackle the difficult uphill portion first, knowing that things will become easier later.

Climbing uphill means thinking of others first. It means putting the interests of others before your own and measuring the value of your words and actions by how much they will help awaken the buddha-nature in the people around you. The way of selflessness is a difficult ascent at first, but it levels out in time to a pleasant boulevard with a satisfying view.

Some people seem to emit the smell of the troubles they have undergone, making them difficult to approach. There are others, however, who have overcome their problems; their buddha-nature shines forth. These are the people with an appealing ambience, with the wisdom to accept the daily routine of life just as it is and to always choose the most human-like way in all things.

Life through Half-Closed Eyes

Our world appears to be a chaotic place, but step back to get a better look and you can see an intricate pattern of balance. Earth revolves around the sun in a fixed orbit; the moon likewise revolves around Earth in an orderly fashion. On our planet, plants absorb the carbon dioxide exhaled by animals, while animals breathe the oxygen exuded by plants. Even the smallest disturbance in this balance jeopardizes the continued existence of all humanity.

Of all the numerous eggs produced by the female codfish, only a very few grow to maturity. How sad, you may muse. But suppose all those eggs were to become adult codfish—the oceans would overflow with them! We refer to the laws of nature and the cosmic order to explain the delicate balance that keeps our universe intact. Similar laws and systems of order apply to human society as well.

Society requires order and harmony to function effectively. You can understand how far off the Way someone has strayed if she lives without giving any consideration at all to those around her, or if she always thinks about things using her own set of standards. Yet it seems to be human nature to become selfish and thoughtless the minute we are left to our own devices. Self-centeredness disrupts balanced relationships and can lead only to self-inflicted wounds. That is why it is so important to practice selflessness and to train ourselves to always think of others first.

It is said that the Buddha is invariably depicted with eyes half-open because he is looking at the external world with half his vision and at his own inner self with the other half. We cannot perceive things as they really are if we contemplate only the external world or only our inner selves. Balance is important. We need to look both inside and outside at the same time. The same is true of our relationships with other people. We achieve balance in human relationships only when our innate, preconditioned self-centeredness gives way to a caring for other people. When we act on this caring, our reward is a wonderful, unexpected joy.

In most business enterprises, the start of a new fiscal year is a time for forging new relationships, as new employees are hired and others are transferred to different departments. After a period of two to six months, personal preferences become clear. All would be well if we liked the people we worked with, but the minute we decide we dislike a coworker or boss, each day at the office becomes a chore rather than a joy. Our surrounding world shrinks with every person we come to dislike.

You will not hear the words of others or be able to read their innermost minds if your own heart is tightly closed against everything coming from outside you. People are quick to sense such an attitude and will soon give up on you. "There is no sense talking to that one," they will say. If you are conciliatory and open-minded, however, you will be able to listen to others and always interpret their words in the best possible light. Interact with others in good faith and they will in time treat you the same way. The harmony you attain with one person will quickly spread to include others.

Progress, whether in the workplace or in society as a whole, is most quickly achieved when we take the initiative to be kind to others and to help them in any way we can. When we give of ourselves we can communicate and grow along with others. Sincere communication brightens the workplace and moves us forward, toward our common goals.

It is a pleasure to be given something good to eat. It is an even greater pleasure to have others reward our efforts with wholehearted praise when we prepare good food for them. We delight in brightening the faces of our children and other family members, even if we ourselves must do without to make them happy. The fulfillment we feel when we make others happy is a special kind of joy that never fades. We all find joy in being needed by others, and when others praise us, our need for recognition is fulfilled; that makes us especially happy. The human need to be recognized is the very core of our existence and a clear indication that we cannot live in isolation.

Where Is Hell?

I noted earlier that the Buddha's half-opened eyes show that he is looking within himself even as he gazes out at the external world. What does it mean to look within oneself? What are we supposed to be looking for?

Buddhism teaches that the world after death is divided into six realms, one of which is hell. In the past, hell was the awful fate that awaited those who did evil. In other words, the threat of hell was a moral incentive to do only good. The Japanese word for hell, *jigoku,* originally referred only to the underworld of the dead. After the Buddhist concept of hell was introduced, however, the ancient Japanese who saw hot steam billowing out of crevices in the earth trembled at the thought of being consigned to the fires and boiling liquid that surely must be the source of the steam. A long time ago, this was enough to deter many a person from evil, but not today.

Today's hell is the hell of the mind. It appears perfectly normal on the surface but seethes with murderous rage underneath. Buddhism teaches that we are trapped within the six realms of existence—in ascending order, hell; the realms of hungry spirits (covetousness), animals (ignorance), *asuras* (disputes), and human beings (normality); and finally, heaven (joy). In Japan, the traditional emphasis on these six realms of existence and our inability to escape their confines has given Buddhism a bleak and gloomy image. I think we need to redefine Buddhism in terms to which contemporary people can better relate and which we can apply to make ourselves better human beings.

The six realms of existence are not mysterious places to which we go after death but exist right now within our own hearts and minds. As the great priest Nichiren said, "Ask where to find heaven and hell and the answer is within our own bodies."

The Dual Self

The world of the hungry spirits resembles the real world, in which those who have plenty are concerned only with filling their own bellies, ignoring the millions all around them who are starving. For a time right after the end of World War II, we Japanese lived on food provided by others. Without this aid we would have starved, yet already we have forgotten it. Now when rice is imported from overseas, we say it does not taste good and throw it away. It is this kind of wasteful and ungrateful attitude that characterizes the hungry spirits of the Buddhist hell.

The next realm of being, that of animals, is an amoral world in which we ignore our own failings and criticize the failings of others. In this realm we are like the sumo wrestler who loses a bout and protests that the ring was too small, or the baseball player who fails to steal second base and grumbles that first and second base were too far apart. Unreasonable complaints and ignoring the rules of the game are characteristics of the animal realm.

The next realm, that of the *asuras,* is a state of constant friction and frustration, a world of unfulfilled desires.

It is said that humanity is the master of all creation. The realm of human beings thus would seem the best place to be. But without support and guidance, human beings are like ships without compasses, drifting wherever the tides and winds take us, being snatched up by the gusts of circumstances, ready at any moment to be pulled back into the lower realms. In the realm of human beings the human mind is always swaying, affected by whatever it encounters.

The realm of heaven is certainly a place of joy, but it is a joy that can be only temporary. It is not like the deep, quiet, and eternal joy that we can gain from the teachings of the Buddha. Joy in the realm of heaven is a fleeting thing, quick to disappear, leaving behind the desolation of the drunkard who awakens from a bout of intoxication.

We bear within ourselves all of these realms, yet we are unaware of their presence. Our hearts and minds are constantly changing with every person we meet, with every event that takes place. To look into ourselves and be able to regard this turmoil with calm and forbearance: that is what it means to look at oneself with half-open eyes.

Take the time to stop and look into yourself. You can do it in front of the household altar or even while you are sitting on a park bench. Stop, say, once a week, to examine yourself with half-open eyes. Ask yourself, "How am I doing these days?

Have I been a bit too unrestrained? Am I being too antagonistic? Have I forgotten how to be sincere?" Do not feel that you have to overcome the turbulence of your six inner realms; we all keep moving among these multiple realms. It is enough just to recognize your own human frailties.

The first of the two characters for the Japanese word *zazen* (meditation) means "to sit." It is an ideograph of two human figures on the ground facing each other. One is the self that is tossed hither and yon by desires; the other is the self that discovers the inner buddha-nature. The dual self "sits" and debates in search of the true way of living. Affluence is not measured by how many things you have attained but by how much calmness you can bring to carrying on this kind of debate with yourself.

CHAPTER 13

SOME THINGS LOST, SOME THINGS GAINED

Mr. Zhao Puchu, president of the Buddhist Association of China, was a fellow member of the World Conference of Religions for Peace and one of my most trusted friends. On my eighty-first birthday, Mr. Zhao presented me with an example of his calligraphy of the Chinese characters that mean *hanju* (half-life) in Japanese. In China, this expression is a felicitous reference to the belief that at the age of 81 a person has lived only half his life. From ages past, it has been widely believed in China that the natural life span of a human being is 162 years. Thus, at 81, we have come only halfway.

I have heard of certain scientific theories that claim that our biological life span is roughly six times the number of years it takes us to attain maturity. Since it takes about fifteen to twenty years for a human being to reach physical maturity, we should be able to live from 90 to 120 years. I suspect we would all like to live that long, ending our lives as naturally as a candle burns down and sputters out, or like a great tree that one day finally falls over.

Unfortunately, most of us are not able to live out our natural life spans. If nothing else, we succumb to the process of aging, which weakens our bodies and erodes our energy. The once robust physique loses its elasticity and wrinkles appear; hair thins; eyes and ears weaken; and the spine begins to bend. As we age, our bodies gradually refuse to do what we want them to.

One of the saddest things about growing old, besides the decline in our physical capabilities, is the way we lose our sense of self. Our position in society is taken away from us and we are compelled to stop working. Our children grow up and leave home. Our health deteriorates. In old age we mourn our losses.

In Japan, the salaried worker first confronts the approach of old age when he reaches retirement and must leave the company in which he has toiled for so long. On retirement we must bid farewell to many things. We say good-bye to the company, to our position in it, to our monthly pay, to the information that was available to us when we were working, and to our coworkers. These farewells are difficult for many people. Why, they wonder, must they let go of everything to which they dedicated their lives? Here Professor Emeritus Akira Tago of Chiba University gives us good advice. Change your perspective, he tells us, and you will see that all these farewells, all these endings, also mark new beginnings. If every encounter is the beginning of a parting, then the reverse is equally true: every parting is the beginning of a new encounter. Losing our title and status, we gain freedom.

And here is the key to a positive approach to aging: think not about what you have lost but about what you have gained. We tend to remember only our highest achievements and take for granted the position, income, and good health we enjoyed at the peak of our working life. It is only because we try to measure everything else against this that we feel such a great sense of loss.

Happiness Waits to Be Discovered

People's downfalls are measured by how far they descend from the social status they once achieved. The Japanese term for downfall is *shikkyaku,* written with the characters meaning "to lose one's footing." A modern-day example is the male corporate executive accustomed to riding in a chauffeur-driven car. The loss of that privilege upon retirement seems very great. But just think of all he has gained! For example, the time he once spent at the company is now free for doing whatever he pleases. Instead of earning an income he can do something he really enjoys.

Certainly, retirees do not have the physical stamina of youth. But they can draw on a rich lode of life experience and the wisdom they thereby attained. Now, at last, they can apply themselves to doing things for others. *Okina* is an honorific term that was once applied to an elderly person who had the wisdom gained from long life-experience and was able to make impartial judgments without personal bias. The truly disinterested elderly person can envelop one and all in a warm embrace that wins everyone's love.

A sense of community is lacking among most contemporary Japanese, but it is clear that community will play an increasingly important role in society. Happiness is not something we have to pursue and capture but can be found here and now; it is only waiting to be discovered. Our social welfare systems have improved. Government and private pensions, together with careful planning for the future, mean that most people should not have to dread the loss of income that results from retirement. Instead of longing for the things we cannot have, we should become less greedy and be content within our limitations. In this spirit, we should be grateful for what we have here and now and be satisfied with making the best of it. This is the recipe for a healthy and simple life that puts quality before quantity.

How to Be Loved by Others

A certain village is known for the longevity of its residents. A study to find the secret of their long lives revealed that the elderly villagers spent each and every day doing things for others. Their primary concern in life was to be useful to other people: their families, their children and grandchildren who had gone off to work in the cities, and their neighbors. Longevity is often attributed to diet. If we eat more kelp and keep our meals simple, we are told, we will add years to our lives. The truth is, however, that the secret of longevity is not so much in our diet as in our worldview.

The way to ensure a long life is to give ungrudgingly of our time and energy, always smile, and offer cheerful greetings to those around us. There are two broad categories of the elderly: the old man or woman who is always smiling and is liked by everyone, and the grouch who is disliked by one and all. The person who is warmly regarded is the one who always puts others first, while the one who is disliked is the selfish person who has lost flexibility.

In his book *Oi e no Chosen* (The Challenge of Growing Old), nursing authority Dr. Shigeaki Hinohara classifies the elderly into four types. The first type is mellow, self-effacing, and open to the ideas of the young. This kind of person is a good advisor and generally attracts admirers. The second type is tense and guarded, as if clad in armor. This kind of elderly person is prone to complain that "things weren't so easy in my day." Such people are set in their ways and are unforgiving of those who even suggest other possibilities. As they get older, they become more tense and guarded. The third type is offended by whatever she sees or hears and is always indignant. These are the old people who are constantly criticizing everything, from the government to today's teenagers. Others tend to keep their distance from people like this. The fourth type is the elderly person who leaves everything up to others and becomes a burden.

What type of elderly person each of us will become depends on our attitude. We can either sit back and decide that others should be doing things for us because we are old or make a positive effort to serve others instead of being served by them. The more we demand, the less satisfied we will be. The self-centered person finds fault with everything, is always irritated, and does nothing but complain.

Clearly, the older we get, the more important positive thinking becomes. This is the key to a fulfilling old age. Our golden years are when we attain maturity as human beings and when we can and should be at our most productive. It is such a waste to fail to savor the rich harvest that is possible in old age. Nothing is so sad as those who demean themselves with unfounded complaints.

Living up to Our Potential

How others treat us depends on how we act. People will not feel very friendly toward someone who is always resentful. But they will respond with gratitude to someone who freely expresses thanks. That is why we must be the first to show that we are grateful. We should look back on the path we have traveled and think about the many, many people whose support made possible a life that we may have thought we built all by ourselves. It is impossible to remain ungrateful once we realize that we owe so much to so many. From this deep-rooted feeling of thanksgiving come humility, kindness, and cheerfulness. Even the disabled and the bedridden can bring joy to the family members who care for them with a simple word of thanks and a smile. The way to measure how happy and fulfilling a person's life has been is, I believe, by the amount of joyful thanksgiving in his heart.

I am told that at the age of sixty the average person has used only one-third of his or her brain. Even the greatest thinkers employ only one-half of their brains at best. In the prime of life, most of us have used only one-fourth of our brains. What a waste! The parts of the body that are not constantly used will atrophy over time. If we do not walk, our leg muscles will wither from disuse. In the same way, our teeth deteriorate when we eat only soft and easily swallowed foods. The person who would rather watch television all the time than attempt to think about things may become senile at an early age. To stay young, we must use our legs, our teeth, and our heads. I have seen many people in their sixties and seventies who continue working hard to serve others. Such people have a special radiance.

Chunda's Offering

It is indeed difficult not to be able to move about as we would like. If our bodies seem to hurt here, there, and everywhere, we will probably be frowning most of the time. Near the end of his life, on his final journey, the Buddha said, "Like an old cart that can be kept operating only with the help of leather thongs, so my body can be kept going only with much help." Not even the Buddha could prevent his physical body from aging. Yet despite his condition, he continued to preach the Dharma right to the end.

The Buddha is said to have died after eating food offered to him by the blacksmith Chunda. Yet he thanked Chunda, saying, "I am not dying because of the food Chunda gave me. My death is the direct result of my birth. The food Chunda offered me had the highest merit." With these words the Buddha sought to deflect criticism from Chunda for causing his death. At the same time, his assertion that his death was the result of his birth was a way of saying that his ties to the world simply had come to an end.

We cannot stop the aging of our bodies. But whether we choose to complain about our gradual decline or to thank family and friends for their support will make all the difference in our world.

How Disease Protects Us

Long-lived people seem to catch colds often. Many are beset by runny noses the minute the weather turns cool. What they do not realize is that a runny nose indicates a sensitivity to the germs in the air, a sign that they have a certain resistance to disease.

As I have said many times, none of us lives in isolation. We exist in relation to many other things. This fact is true of society as a whole and of our individual physical beings. From outside our bodies we take in the food, air, and light essential to life and expel what we do not need. Our continued existence depends on the constant repetition of this cycle. It is important, therefore, that we have the flexibility to adapt to changes in our environment.

The human body is made up of a multitude of cells that are constantly dividing, disappearing, and reemerging. Each of these cells reacts to and changes along with the changes taking place in other cells. As one authority has noted, "Every life form is part of an open system in which it takes in, expels, and exchanges all the rest of nature."

It is wrong to assume that we exist independently of our surroundings. Our inner and outer worlds are one and the same. Injury, pain, and suffering occur when the delicate interaction of our inner and outer worlds is disturbed. Disease is a warning sign that the cycle of exchange has been broken and needs repair.

No one enjoys getting sick. The fear of illness becomes especially acute as we grow older. But becoming sick is the body's way of trying to cure itself; we should respond accordingly. Not for us is the tranquil, uneventful security of a sterile environment. Our stability is the result of a constant effort to adapt to change. Note the expert skiers who keep their knees bent and maintain their stability on even the bumpiest and steepest inclines. Bent knees are important in the world of sumo wrestling, too. The wrestler who stays low, with his feet firmly planted, is more likely to win the match. Bent knees make it possible to respond quickly to whatever technique one's opponent may employ. In contrast, the wrestler who remains rigidly upright is easily felled.

CHAPTER 14

WE DIE TO BE BORN ANEW

Throughout history, human beings have sought a cure for aging and death. We have never questioned the notion that surely it would be wonderful to be able to live forever. Yet our values, even the very meaning of life, would be completely different if there were no such thing as death. Without the possibility of death ever before us, how much would we value each day, each moment, of our existence? By the same token, how much would we enjoy certain foods if we could have them any time we wanted?

We take the air we breathe and the water we drink for granted, giving little thought to how essential they are to life. Only when we risk losing these elements do we realize how important they are to us. The same holds true for life. It glows with promise because death is inevitable. We would be unlikely to regret time wasted if time were available in unlimited supply. But life is limited, so precious time flows through our fingers. Sad to say, most of us never make the best use of the time we have and die unfulfilled.

Even if we were to live forever and never die, at each moment we would still be unable to decide what to do. Human life has a limit, an expiration date; that fact is always in our minds, even unconsciously. For this reason we try so furiously to learn what is of the utmost importance to us, or even why we are alive.

When we find the answer and do our best to live as we think we should, then we can welcome death with no regrets about things we left undone. We should live each day keeping in mind that our lives must come to an end sometime. It is when we acknowledge the inevitability of death that we are able to see what is truly important and what is not. Only then can we know how we should be living.

Put Your Best Foot Forward

Life seems meaningless to the person who equates existence with the physical body. But for the person who sees the death of the physical body as rebirth into another existence, life has great significance, and every minute of his present existence becomes precious.

We live out our individual lives to the fullest in order to pass on eternal life. Each of us is like a runner in a long-distance relay race—we strive to run our best so that we can pass the baton to the next runner. One of the Chinese classics notes that each season has its time and place. Spring gives way to summer, summer to autumn, autumn to winter, and so on, as each season completes its assigned task. People who have attained success but then keep pursuing it further and further may be going against the dictates of nature.

Birth, aging, illness, and death are the tasks we have been assigned. Our lives are fulfilled when we apply ourselves to each of those tasks with diligence. Each individual life is a link in the chain of eternal life. Do not consider your last years a downhill trek. Rather think of them as a march upward to death and eternity.

Do What Can Be Done Today

Mother Teresa of Calcutta, a recipient of the Nobel Peace Prize, dedicated her life to the care of hopelessly ill, impoverished, and homeless people. Motion picture director Shigeki Chiba, who made a film about her life, said, "As I edited the film, I came to realize that I had never seen such a beautiful person as this little wrinkled old woman." He said that he was most impressed by the spirituality she could convey even when viewed from behind. The people for whom Mother Teresa cared all said that she made them feel loved by God and confident that God heard their prayers. The last words of those who died in her arms often were, "I am glad that I was born into this world."

Shugoro Yamamoto (1903–1967), a popular novelist, had this to say about death: "Death is not a disappearance from this world, but proof of a person's existence. Death finishes off life; it is a completion. It is not extinction, but completion."

When we are confident that our lives will be passed on eternally, we can bid farewell to this world in peace, saying, "I shall be reborn. I shall come again." In the Majjhima Nikaya (Middle-Length Sayings) the Buddha left us these words:

The past should not be followed after, the future not desired.
What is past is got rid of and the future has not come.
But whoever has vision now here, now there, of a present
    thing,
Knowing that it is immovable, unshakable, let him cultivate
    it.

Swelter at the task this very day. Who knows whether he will
   die tomorrow?
There is no bargaining with the great hosts of Death.
Thus abiding ardently, unwearied day and night,
He indeed is "Auspicious" called, described as a sage at
   peace.

CHAPTER 15

DO YOU HEAR THE CRIES OF THE WORLD?

In a famous Kabuki play, the hero receives a financial windfall. "What an auspicious *engi!*" he declares as he strikes a dramatic pose. The term *engi* refers to luck or destiny, and the Japanese frequently use it. *Engi* is also the most basic of the Buddha's teachings. According to the concept of *engi,* everything arises because of everything else. The Buddha used a simile to illustrate the point: Two bundles of reeds can stand upright because they are leaning against each other. Take away one bundle and the other will fall. This is because that is, and that is because this is.

Each of us is a bundle of reeds. We think we stand on our own and are confused when we are forced to realize that we do not. Because of the working of *engi,* or dependent origination, all things arise, continue to exist, change, and eventually cease to exist. In other words, the entire world, including our own existence, is founded on the three characteristics of the Dharma: everything is impermanent, all things are devoid of self, and nirvana is quiescence. It is through *engi* that everything arises and is extinguished; in this context we can also refer to *engi* as "encounters." No one is automatically good or bad. According to Buddhism, a person becomes good or bad through good encounters with others or through bad encounters with others.

This idea implies that, to create a better society, we should take it upon ourselves to bring about as many good encounters as possible. Without improving society as a whole, we cannot expect to secure happiness for ourselves. That is why it is important to start with our own individual encounters, making an effort to ensure that they are good encounters. This is the Way of the bodhisattva. The many bodhisattvas who appear in the Lotus Sutra are our role models. In Japan, one of the best-known and most-beloved of these bodhisattvas is Kannon (Avalokiteshvara). Kannon is the Regarder of the Cries of the World, especially sensitive to people's cries of sadness, their moans of unhappiness, and their wailing for salvation, and offers succor and compassion in a variety of forms tailored to each individual.

Like Kannon, we too can offer a helping hand to others, to each person in the form most appropriate to his need. You cannot stand on a high platform and expect to guide others only through your words. Only when you stand on the same ground as those you hope to lead to goodness, only when you think and feel as others do, only when you act with them will they be willing to listen to you. Kannon is a role model for how best to help others. Another way to think of Kannon is to see him as the embodiment of the buddha-nature that exists in each and every one of us. We can never attain Kannon's perfection, but we can strive to come as close as possible so that we can, in even small ways, assist in Kannon's acts of compassion.

Compassion Comes from Empathy

People who do not have free use of their limbs suffer all kinds of inconvenience. Inconvenience, however, is not the same thing as unhappiness. We were all totally helpless at one time in our lives. We had to be held and fed and in every way depended on others to care for us when we were infants. Many of us will once again require the same kind of care when we grow old. So you see, no one goes through life without at some point experiencing some inconvenience and dependence upon others.

A human being is capable of many things. Some of us excel at rapid calculation, others have phenomenal memories or great eloquence, and still others can run quickly. There is no end to the possibilities. But perhaps one of the most important human capabilities is the ability to reflect upon the self. Only people who can see themselves with an objective eye can empathize with the feelings of others.

In his "Seventeen-Article Constitution," Prince Shotoku (574–622) said that, since we are all ordinary people, "We are all one with another, wise and foolish, like 'ear-gold,' which has no end." What he described as "ear-gold" must surely be a round golden earring that has no beginning and no end. We tend to want to separate the talented from the not-so-talented, for some reason assuming that the former are superior. But just because one person has more capabilities than another does not mean that that person is better than any other. If we are all part of the unbroken mesh of life, there is no way to place one person before another.

Better the filled cup than the empty wine bottle. The important thing is that we use to the fullest the capabilities that we do have. The compassionate person wishes for the happiness of everyone, without discriminating. Compassion is at once the wish to make others happy and the desire to take away their pain and suffering. Compassion is sensitivity and caring. It is not difficult to master this emotion. Help the person who is lost find her way. On buses and trains, give up your seat to the elderly. Even such small acts of kindness constitute the practice of compassion. One can also be compassionate by comforting and supporting the parent who is worried about a child's wayward behavior or a couple that is on the verge of divorce. We can demonstrate our compassion in such cases by helping others not only to unburden themselves of their pain and suffering but also to cleanse their souls so that they can find new ways to live meaningful and happy lives. This is the ultimate expression of compassion, the ultimate act of bodhisattva caring.

Getting Our Bearings

"Who am I? Where am I?" are the kinds of questions that many a young person has been tempted to ask in the confusion of growing up in the bustle of contemporary society. The teachings of Buddhism can answer such queries.

Zen Buddhism consists of three important elements. The first is seated meditation, or *zazen,* when the meditator looks into herself to discover her buddha-nature and encounter her real self.

The second important element is *takuhatsu,* or begging for alms, in which the Zen practitioner goes from house to house. By going out into the world this way, one meets all kinds of people and learns much. A certain religious sect has even said that if one wants to know God, one must beg like this. Another relevant comment was made by the renowned novelist Eiji Yoshikawa (1892–1962), who declared that all people were his teachers. Yoshikawa must surely have interacted with a great many people and learned much from them, for the stories he has left us are indeed wonderful. Another great artist, the late film comedian Charlie Chaplin, claimed that the street corner was his school. I understand what he meant: encounters with people have always been important in my life, too.

The third important element of Zen Buddhism is *samu,* or the daily chores of temple life. As one weeds the temple grounds and cultivates the temple garden, one comes to realize how dependent we are on nature.

Thus, we encounter the self through *zazen,* we encounter others through *takuhatsu,* and we encounter nature through *samu.* Zen shows the Way to seek the answers to the questions "Where did I come from?" "What am I doing?" and "Where am I going?"

News reports tell us that every year more than ten thousand people in Japan die from overwork. The kanji character for *busy* is written with the character meaning "heart" and the character meaning "to die." People in business today are so busy that their hearts die. Also, when people are extremely busy they tend to forget the self in the confusion of work. The Japanese word describing this kind of confusion, *awateru,* is written with the character for "heart" and another character meaning "to become barren."

Is it right to be so busy? So busy that we have no time to contemplate the beauty of the flowers that tell of the changing seasons? So busy that we have no eyes for the sparkle of the fresh young leaves on the trees as they glint in the sun? So busy that we think only of racing from one assignment to the next? Work is certainly important, but is it not equally important to find some quiet time each day to look into the self?

It is when we look within ourselves that we become aware of the many kindnesses we have received from others, and out of this awareness comes a feeling of gratitude. The joy of having done something good fills our whole being. Every good deed enhances our character and the way we live, even though we may not be aware of it. To put it another way, every good deed fosters the growth of our buddha-nature and gives it more luster. The more initiative we take to live and work for the good of others, the greater is our joy. And the greater our inner joy, the closer we come to the Buddha.

Make others happy and you will expand your own heart and mind in a way that will radically change the way you perceive things. This practice can be habit-forming; strive each day to do good for others and eventually you will find yourself always working for the happiness of others.

Rights and Privileges

The Japanese word for a "right" or "privilege," *kenri,* used to be written with the character meaning "reasonable" or "just." Today, however, it is written with the character meaning "benefit" or "profit." There is a subtle but important difference in the two ways of writing the word: the former implies an authority with a reasonable rationale, while the latter emphasizes personal gain or advantage. I believe that the old-fashioned rendition of *kenri* better reflects the true meaning of the word, in the same way that a *right* in English implies a privilege founded on correct reasoning. In an era when just about everyone seems to be clamoring for his or her "rights," I think it is wise to consider the true meaning of the term. Rights are won only after fulfilling certain responsibilities. Chapter III, Article 13 of the Japanese Constitution states: "All people shall be respected as individuals." What tends to be forgotten is the passage that follows: "to the extent that it does not interfere with the public welfare." Freedom means responsibility. A democracy of people intent only on fulfilling their own individual desires is likely to degenerate into chaotic mob rule.

When the Buddha was dying, his disciples wept and asked, "What will sustain us after you are gone?" The Buddha replied, "Depend not on others, but on the guiding light of yourself." And he continued, "Let the Dharma be a lamp unto you." Without the light of the Dharma, right will conflict with right, and ego with ego. A common complaint today is that people are selfish, thinking only of themselves. This state of affairs exists because many people still have yet to experience the joy of working for others instead of only for their own interests. You cannot make your life worthwhile just by thinking about it. You experience fulfillment only when you do something for the benefit of someone else, when you offer a helping hand to others. There is great pleasure to be had in helping someone in trouble, in lending a sympathetic ear to another's woes, in being thanked by someone for something you have done. Acting to make others happy: that is the shortest route to achieving one's own happiness.

Losing Sight of the Self

Our obsession with our individual profit or loss prevents us from seeing or hearing what is really important. Certainly, it can be a great annoyance to others when someone is oblivious to his or her own responsibility within a group. But even more important, inattentive or insensitive people are a danger to themselves.

The following episode appears in the *Chuang-tzu*, a Chinese literary work of the fourth century BCE. One day Chuang-tzu was walking in the woods, with bow and arrow in hand. Suddenly a magpie flew in front of him and stopped on a chestnut tree. "Ah," thought Chuang-tzu, "here is something I can catch." He held his breath and carefully approached the magpie. But the magpie made no move to fly away. It was intently looking at something else. Chuang-tzu looked closely and saw that the magpie's attention was riveted on a praying mantis. The praying mantis, in turn, was equally still, concentrating on a cicada making a singing sound farther along the tree branch. Chuang-tzu gasped and swallowed. The cicada continued making its shrill sound, totally unaware that its life was in danger. The praying mantis was so intent on catching the cicada that it failed to notice the magpie behind it. And the magpie was so determined to pounce on the praying mantis that it was completely oblivious of Chuang-tzu. This sight put Chuang-tzu in a philosophical mood. How foolish, he thought, to focus so thoroughly on what is right before your eyes that you lose all sight of the danger you yourself are in. All of a sudden, his reverie was rudely interrupted: "Who goes there? Don't you know that it is forbidden to enter this chestnut grove?" Chuang-tzu had been caught by the keeper of the grove. Chuang-tzu writes of his shame and embarrassment. He had been pitying the insects and birds he came upon without realizing that he himself was trespassing.

How often has each of us done the same kind of thing? Perhaps we should look into our own hearts first before we laugh at the folly of others. Putting others before ourselves is the fastest way to gain an objective perspective on the self. The spirit of helping others, being kind to others, or making others happy is really the spirit of forgetting the self and striving for the benefit of others. Perfect purity and perfect innocence are nothing but the sincere desire to be useful to others, to be kind to others, and to make others happy. Buddhism teaches us that to save others by guiding them to the Dharma is like ferrying them across a river to the other side, the side of happiness. A fragment of poetry describes this kind of selfless giving:

Cross again and again to ferry others to the other side,
Yourself never disembarking to climb the river bank.

Acting Here and Now

The uncertainty of tomorrow leads some of us to rely on oracles and other people to take a happy-go-lucky stance: what will be will be. The Bible tells us not to worry about tomorrow. Tomorrow's worries will take care of themselves; it is enough to worry about today. Shakyamuni also taught that the important thing is to think about what can be done here and now. A saying in the *Dento-roku* (Record of the Transmission of the Lamp) goes, "The self always exists here fully," which means that we should live with integrity and to the fullest at all times and in all places. The Buddhist concept of karma tends to be viewed as a fearful thing, as atonement in the present for the sins of a past life. But when Shakyamuni spoke of karma, he was referring to the actions we should be taking right here and now.

Everyone wants to do good. Anyone who sees pictures of starving children in Africa, for example, becomes uneasy at the painful sight. Something must be done, we feel. But then we think that no one person can possibly cope with all the troubles of the world. Very quickly the urge to do something fades and we lose interest. It helps if someone urges us on to specific action, saying, for example, "Let us save the starving children by forgoing an occasional meal and instead use the money to help these people," or "Let us each give one blanket to protect people from the cold." It is a lot easier to do something when we unite our forces. Working as a group, we can fully harness the potential of each individual. Yes, one person can make a difference.

The Merit of Not Hurrying

When I was sixteen years old, I left my hometown of Tokamachi in Niigata Prefecture to go to Tokyo. My father's advice at that time was: "Tokyo has many earthquakes. If a quake strikes, do not panic. You will be laughed at as a country bumpkin. Just drink some water and calm down." Lo and behold, on my fourth day in the big city, the Great Kanto Earthquake of 1923 struck. We heard the tiles slide off the roof in a great rush. My companions were on the verge of panic. But I recalled my father's words. I did not want to be laughed at. I took a sip of water to calm my nerves and then said to the others, "Calm down; don't panic." Working together, we were able to gather nearly all of our valuables and escape the chaos. Later I heard that some people, in their rush to flee, brought with them strange things for which they had no use. One person grabbed a pile of diapers. My boss at the time thanked me for keeping a level head in the crisis. My father's advice had helped me remain unruffled during great confusion. A splash of cold water is less of a shock if you know that it is coming.

The Buddha's teachings of impermanence and nonself help us be prepared. Keep these teachings in mind and it becomes easier and easier to get through each day. I hear that in the 1995 Great Hanshin Earthquake in Kobe, buildings crumbled in an instant; the impact was twice as strong as in Tokyo seventy-two years earlier. Yet even in the midst of terror, the victims retained their humanity. Said one person in a television interview, "My wife broke her leg. I want to thank whomever it was who carried her all the way to the hospital. He left without even telling us his name. There are still some decent people in this country." Yes, there are still some people in this world who will help others without expecting anything in return. Saints are often characterized as being aloof from society and the everyday cares of the world. But I believe that the real saints are in our midst, living as ordinary people.

Chapter 16

Knowing What Is Enough

Happiness depends to a great extent on how one perceives things. Consider the man in his sixties who has for many years now taken care of his bedridden elderly mother. She is more than eighty years old and can do nothing for herself. Her son feeds and washes her and changes her undergarments. But this man says, "How wonderful to be blessed again with a child at my age! I consider caring for my mother a privilege for which I am most grateful."

I remember being greatly moved by these words, stated so matter-of-factly. Every time I meet a selfless person like this, I wonder, When and how did he learn to be so caring? What kind of childhood did he have? How was he raised by his parents? Such people would answer that there was nothing particularly special about their backgrounds. They grew up seeing their parents give of themselves. By the time they became adults, the same giving spirit was deeply ingrained in their personalities.

Our perception of things profoundly affects the way we see the world. What child, dressed in freshly laundered clothes, stays clean for very long? Do you become angry at the child for getting dirty "again" or do you think to yourself how wonderful it is that your child can play with such energy and joy? If you are a housewife, do you complain that your husband's shirts are always getting ragged at the cuffs or do you consider this a sign of how hard he works every day? The difference between the two perceptions is the difference between chronic frustration and constant joy.

We take so much for granted. We consider it a matter of course that in traditional families the husbands will work hard at the office every day, the children will go to school, and the mothers will keep the home spick-and-span. When it becomes dark, we switch on a light; when we want water, we turn on a faucet.

Sengai, an eighteenth-century priest at the temple Shofuku-ji in Hakata, Kyushu, was noted for his excellent calligraphy and paintings. He was also a fine educator. A number of interesting stories about Sengai have come down to us.

One New Year's Day, a man rushed in to see him, crying, "Help! The couple next door are having a terrible fight and no one can stop them."

"Now, why would they be fighting so on New Year's Day?" Sengai asked.

"It seems the wife overcooked the New Year's stew and that made the husband angry."

"Ah," said Sengai, "now that is a happy thing!"

"Why do you say that having a fight on New Year's Day is a happy thing?" asked the puzzled neighbor.

"Of course it is. Just think—if the wife were sick in bed, it would be impossible for her to fight. The same would be true if the husband were sick. It would be equally impossible if either of them had died; the one still living would not have a partner to fight with! They are able to fight because they are both healthy. So you see, that is a wonderful thing."

What others see as trouble, Sengai saw as something to be grateful for, it is all in the way we decide to look at things. A slight shift in attitude can completely change one's view. Will you see things in a spirit of thanksgiving or will you insist on transferring your dissatisfaction to everything you see?

I used to complain about my wife's slowness in getting ready whenever we were to go out. But my wife has died and now there is no one I can tell to hurry. Sengai was so very right when he said we should be grateful that a wife and husband can still fight.

Losing Can Enrich Your Life

A Japanese saying goes: "Neither a folding screen nor a business can stand without bending." One way to interpret this maxim is that we should be willing to bend the rules a bit once in a while if we hope to succeed in business. Another interpretation is that the business person should strive to bend to the customer's will.

It seems that in recent years in Japan, the former interpretation has held sway. The rules have not been just bent; more often they have been broken. For example, during the bubble economy of the 1980s, certain people and companies were able to borrow large sums of money from the banks without having to put up any kind of security. They used the money to buy land and then let the land sit idle until they could sell it for a very tidy profit. Seeing such activities, some other people were ready to give up trying to earn an honest living, considering it a waste of their time and energy. The bubble has now burst, however, and these days all we hear about are people and companies burdened with land they cannot sell and loans they cannot possibly repay. Business, many now agree, is best conducted honestly.

There are still people who think that anything goes as long as they can turn a profit. In the same way, some athletes are willing to risk grave physical damage by taking performance-enhancing drugs so that they can win no matter what. If profit is the only gauge of success, then an ordinary salaried worker can hardly be called successful. But if the worker is measured by how much joy and happiness he or she has been able to give to others, then true success is possible for everyone.

Junzo Sekine, former manager of the Yakult Swallows baseball team, once said, "When you compete, of course you compete to win. But it is impossible to win every single game. When it comes to life in general, winning is by no means everything. In fact, life is enriched by an occasional loss; our memories are all the more precious because we sometimes lose."

Rich Yet Hungry Spirits

The hungry spirits of the Buddhist hells are called *pretas* in Sanskrit. They are always starving and thirsty. According to Buddhist teaching, there are three kinds of hungry spirits in our world. The first is the impoverished hungry spirit who can never get enough to eat and who has no wealth to speak of. The many violent conflicts around the world today are increasing the population of poor hungry spirits. These spirits are to be pitied.

The second kind is the hungry spirit who manages to subsist. This type of spirit is able to get some food, though not three full meals every day. These spirits, too, are to be pitied.

The third kind is the wealthy hungry spirit who has more than enough to eat every day and enjoys great riches. The wealthy hungry spirits of our world own cars and houses and know what is going on through their television sets. But even though they see images of starving children around the world, they feel nothing. I think that Japan today has an especially large population of wealthy hungry spirits.

In the sixth century, the Indian Buddhist priest Bodhidharma is said to have been warmly welcomed to China by Emperor Wu (502–549) of the Liang dynasty, who had recently converted to Buddhism. The emperor said to Bodhidharma, "I have accumulated many merits by building temples and encouraging the education of Buddhist clerics. What will be my reward?" Bodhidharma replied, "There is no reward."

There are indeed many merits in building temples, training priests, and spreading Buddhist teachings far and wide. But all this work is for naught if it is done in expectation of a reward. A pure and detached heart is required. Doing good is its own reward. "What more could you want?" Bodhidharma seems to be saying. Many people perform good deeds, not simply for the act itself, but to satisfy their own desires or to gain fame. These kinds of people may not deserve a reward; yet they are preferable, I think, to the wealthy hungry spirits who do nothing at all. Even if one is originally motivated by selfish desire, the repetition of good acts can eventually become rewarding in itself.

An Era of Contentment

While there are still some Buddhist temples that adhere to a strict vegetarian diet, most no longer limit what may be eaten. Whatever we eat, we need to be aware that much plant and animal life has been sacrificed to sustain our existence. Our foremost desire should be to make our own lives equally of use to others; offering to help others is a human obligation. The ancient Japanese never failed to express their thanks to the shellfish that were a major part of their diet. The great shell mounds of more than ten thousand years ago testify to this tradition. These mounds were not refuse piles but monuments to the shellfish lives that had been sacrificed to feed human beings.

As the contentious twentieth century drew to a close, many people hoped that the twenty-first century would be one of sharing. Humanity will not survive otherwise. A group of fifteen must gladly share ten loaves of bread. We need to strive for what Buddhism calls knowing contentment with little. Multiply one hundred by zero and all you get is zero. You may enjoy great wealth and have many possessions, but if you lack the spirit of thanksgiving, all this wealth is as nothing and you will never be satisfied.

There can be no future for the human race if we continue to rush about trying to satisfy insatiable desires. We tend to assume that the so-called food crisis is a concern only of developing countries. But the U.S. government recently reported that if we continue to consume at the present rate, a global food crisis will arise within only forty or fifty years. We need to train ourselves to know when enough is enough. Lao-tzu said that the person who knows what is enough will prosper. The Sutra of Legacy Teachings says that the person who knows enough enjoys wealth, pleasure, and peace. Even Saint Paul tells us, "I have learned to be satisfied with what I have" (Phil. 4:11).

The sages have been telling us to know what is enough since ages past. I believe there is no more appropriate time than now to take this teaching to heart.

Chapter 17

Transcending Differences among Religions

Shakyamuni attained enlightenment after carefully observing the people and rich natural environment around him. It is said that what he achieved cannot be expressed in words but can be understood only through much study and training. All religions, however, resort to words to some extent to explain their tenets. The parable is one common tool they use to convey religious truths.

Naturally, these parables are molded by their environment; the religious parables of a desert country are quite different from those born of a lush, green climate. It is not surprising that the concept of transmigration evolved in a humid jungle setting, where the leaves and fruits of trees fall to fertilize the soil and give rise to new trees and new fruit.

When Buddhism was introduced into China and Japan, Buddhist teachers used the cycles of nature to convey their teachings. They explained the mysteries and truths of the sutras in terms of nature. Flowers bloom naturally at the advent of spring. Butterflies go from flower to flower, drinking their nectar and carrying the flowers' pollen from place to place. There is no special agreement between the flowers and the butterflies, yet each fulfills a role.

Saicho, founder of the Tendai sect of Japanese Buddhism, once noted that a net with only one square of mesh is of no use in capturing a bird. In the same way, humanity cannot be saved by one doctrine alone. Many religions are needed to reach as many people as possible. Only when all religions cooperate will it be possible for humanity to find true happiness.

The different religions have many similarities. On some occasions Christian parables better explain a certain doctrine than those of Buddhism. At other times we may recognize that much of Christian teaching is similar to Buddhist doctrine. Personally, I have no qualms about quoting from the scriptures of other religions.

The many religions that exist around the globe developed from specific climatic conditions, cultures, and ethnic characteristics, as well as from the particular needs of their times. Some people feel that all religions are diverse interpretations of the same essential truth. Different religions use different names for the Deity, such as God or the Eternal Buddha, yet in the final analysis I think they all refer to the same great life force that enables the entire universe to exist. (I use the word *God* here loosely to refer to all kinds of gods: those with humanlike personalities and those without; the monotheistic god or a multiplicity of gods; the god or gods close to humans and those that are aloof and distant.)

The Japanese term *shukyo* is written with the character for "immutable truth" and the one for "teaching," thus implying a teaching of truth in a manner that suits the talents of the people of different times, different climates, and different eras. *Shukyo* is the Japanese translation of *religion*, but the two words are not identical in meaning. The Japanese word has deeper and more complex implications than the English one. The teaching inherent in *shukyo* changes with the times, its doctrines and theories increasing all the while. No religion stays the same over a long period of time. Some scholars assert that traces of Zoroastrian belief can be found in Judaism and Christianity. The names of Jewish prophets and of Jesus also appear in the Qur'an.

Certainly, Christianity, Buddhism, and Islam are not one and the same; each has its own particular character. Nevertheless, no one religion, no matter how superior it is considered to be, has a monopoly on truth. Given this fact, it would be best for the different religions of the world to support and cooperate with each other.

A point of view commonly expressed at various international religious conferences is that Christianity and Islam are offshoots of Judaism, while Buddhism is an offshoot of Hinduism. It is high time that we resolve the contradiction of religions' preaching love while criticizing each other at the same time. Let us be magnanimous and strive to enlighten one another. That is my hope as I promote the World Conference of Religions for Peace; it is also the source of my energy.

Happy Is the Peacemaker

Global peace cannot be achieved by one nation alone. Everyone knows that peace is possible only if all people around the world work together to achieve it. But national pride is not easily relinquished, so it is very difficult for all nations to cooperate in the interest of peace. No matter how hard one may strive for world peace, the fruits of one's labors are not immediately apparent. But that does not mean we should stop our efforts.

As Dr. Johan Galtung, the world-renowned authority on peace studies, has said, just because there is no war does not mean that there is peace. Equating peace with the lack of war is like pronouncing a person healthy because there are no visible superficial signs of illness.

There was heated debate in Japan the first time the Japanese Self-Defense Forces took part in United Nations peacekeeping operations (PKOs) a few years ago. I think that religious Japanese have more to hope for in participation by nongovernmental organizations (NGOs) in peacemaking operations (PMOs). For this effort, we need people who are not constrained by issues of profit or loss, willing to give their time and money and expect nothing in return. With leaders like that, others will surely follow. Those who can dedicate themselves totally to the peace effort will surely come to know the highest joy there is. And perhaps we ourselves will be among such people.

When I went to Belgium in 1974 to take part in the second general assembly of the World Conference of Religions for Peace, I was asked by a reporter from a Brussels broadcasting station, "Mr. Niwano, do you really believe that global peace can be realized through this kind of conference?" I replied: "World peace is a very elusive goal. But that is exactly why I am here expending every effort [to achieve it]."

Mother Teresa was once asked a similar question by a reporter: "Could you achieve more if you could use politics to help people?" She replied, "I try to help the person before me. Then I help the next person. That is all." Helping the individual right in front of her was Mother Teresa's way of serving God.

The fifth general assembly of the World Conference of Religions for Peace was held at Monash University in the suburbs of Melbourne, Australia, in January 1989. I was asked to give the opening remarks, and I decided to quote a poem by the Japanese sculptor and poet Kotaro Takamura (1883–1956).

> The fruit before the flower,
> The sprout before the seed,
> Summer before spring.
> Do not accept what does not stand to reason,
> What is obviously unnatural.

In our eagerness to achieve our goals we often long for the sprout to appear before the seed. But if we truly desire peace, we must begin by planting the seeds of peace and carefully tending them. The way to peace is a difficult one and there are no shortcuts. We must make our way as best we can.

Honest to a Fault?

Sincerity and kindness are two forces that will always win recognition in the long run and wield great influence. Having come through more than ninety years of life myself, I can say for certain how true that is. We tread an unbeaten path. First, I lead the way and then those who endorse my views follow. More follow them and together we create a new road. Sincerity and kindness are essential in pioneering new avenues.

The honest person is often laughed at for being a fool. "Honest to a fault," we say about such people. During the years of Japan's bubble economy, the person who worked single-mindedly day in and day out was sometimes labeled a fool. Riches were for the bold and the shrewd, not for the plodders. Somewhere along the line our values became skewed. To my mind, you cannot believe in other people unless you yourself are honest. If you tell lies and are always trying to outwit others, you inevitably will assume that everyone else is also a liar and trickster. You will never be able to enjoy true friendship.

What does it matter whether someone tricks you? How many times have I endeavored to help someone, only to have that person turn on me? In the long run, however, such people narrow the scope of their own world and end up with no one to whom they can turn. You cannot achieve great things if you are constantly thinking only of the bottom line. Great people are those who can laugh at being duped. If genuine laughter is not possible, at least one can wear a smile. Believe in yourself; nothing is more reassuring. My grandfather used to say, "If you trick others, you will cause trouble, but if you are tricked, the only victim is yourself."

Yoshikata Tsukamoto, president of Wacoal, one of Japan's leading lingerie makers, once noted that the truly honest person is responsible for her own actions and so can accept whatever results she brings about. It is the dishonest person who is most taken aback and shamed by failure or loss.

Surely everyone in this world wishes to be happy. But interpretations of exactly what constitutes happiness vary widely. There is no such thing as the essential substance of happiness. What, then, makes us feel happy? Only when we are able to answer this question truthfully can we avoid the disappointment and chronic dissatisfaction that come from chasing after false hopes.

Most people think of happiness as something concrete, almost like something that can be held in their hands. I like to think of happiness, however, as something that we awaken to or become aware of. Happiness is everywhere around us if we only open our eyes and look for it. Humdrum daily life may seem boring, but what joy there is in being able to feel grateful for going from one day to the next without mishap. Happiness depends on one's perception of things.

The word *buddha* means "a person who has awakened." Ordinary people are potential buddhas who have yet to awaken. Buddhism thus embraces the teachings of the Buddha as well as the teachings on how to become a buddha. Inherent in all of us is this potential—our buddha-nature. Life is the opportunity we are given to awaken to the buddha-nature within ourselves. Because life is a steady accumulation of one day upon the next, the key to our happiness is how we conduct ourselves each and every day.

Sato Issai (1772–1859), the Confucian scholar of the late Edo period (1600–1868), said, "Suppose that you are walking in the darkness of night with only one lantern. Fear not the darkness. Make the one lantern your sole guide." We should consider what our one light is. A common expression in the world of Japanese politics is, "One step ahead lies darkness." The wiles of politics are not exactly the same as the darkness that we must battle as individuals, but the unexpected inconsistencies we confront are much the same.

Something that can withstand the strongest wind, that remains solid even though the earth may shake, that will not burn and cannot be washed away, that cannot be attained through the pursuit of tangible things: this is what the ancient sages sought when they removed themselves from the desires of the world and went deep into the mountains to concentrate on religious practices. The male or female monastic who lives a cloistered life is seeking the essence of purity. Such a life renounces society. But if we all chose voluntarily to leave the secular world, society could no longer function. I believe that we can serve the same purpose equally well by entering the world as by leaving it.

The search for truth requires a pure and undefiled heart. Yet even if we are ready to prepare ourselves to leave society behind, we should be equally willing to plunge in and apply in our daily lives the wisdom and insight we have gained. In practical terms, it is important to consider the workplace a training hall for making oneself a better person. The weekends can be a time to refresh the spirit at home or among fellow members of a religious community in preparation for the following week of toil. In modern times, I think this is the replacement for the cloistered life as a way to pursue one's religious growth and live with the bodhisattva spirit in the context of the secular world. After all, it is the Buddha's wish that we apply the truths of transience and nonself in our daily lives, cheerfully and happily, always with thanksgiving. We must live never forgetting what it is that can cause us to lose our humanity.

We must not become complacent when things go well but must always remember to cultivate our hearts and minds. What is most important is the way we choose to lead our own lives.